Skills Worksheet

Directed Reading A

AF344477

Section: Ionic and Covalent Compounds

______ **1.** What is the force of attraction that holds atoms or ions together called?

    a. valence electrons   **c.** chemical bond
    b. ionic compounds   **d.** compound cement

______ **2.** What are the electrons found in the outermost energy levels of an atom called?

    a. valence electrons   **c.** covalent electrons
    b. ionic electrons   **d.** compound electrons

IONIC COMPOUNDS AND THEIR PROPERTIES

______ **3.** An ionic bond is an attraction between

    a. positively charged ions.   **c.** negatively charged ions.
    b. oppositely charged ions.   **d.** metallic ions.

______ **4.** When a metal meets a nonmetal, electrons are transferred and the metal atoms become

    a. positively charged.   **c.** negatively charged.
    b. neutral.   **d.** oppositely charged.

______ **5.** When a metal meets a nonmetal, the nonmetal atom becomes

    a. positively charged.   **c.** negatively charged.
    b. neutral.   **d.** oppositely charged.

______ **6.** Table salt is formed when an electron is transferred from a sodium atom to a

    a. metal atom.   **c.** nonmetal atom.
    b. chlorine atom.   **d.** positively charged atom.

______ **7.** Ionic compounds tend to be brittle solids

    a. at room temperature.   **c.** outdoors.
    b. at high temperatures.   **d.** when wet.

______ **8.** In a crystal lattice each ion is bonded to the

    a. pattern it is made with.   **c.** compound around it.
    b. ions around it.   **d.** crystal's edge.

______ **9.** When an ionic compound is hit, the pattern shifts, ions repel each other and the crystal

    a. becomes more solid.   **c.** breaks apart.
    b. forms a new lattice.   **d.** becomes bonded.

Directed Reading A *continued*

______**10.** Because strong ionic bonds hold ions together, ionic compounds have
   a. a low melting point.   **c.** a high melting point.
   b. a lukewarm melting point.   **d.** a variable melting point.

______**11.** Many ionic compounds dissolve easily
   a. in air.   **c.** in water.
   b. at high temperatures.   **d.** in electric current.

12. When an ionic compound dissolves in water, why can it conduct electric current?

____

____

COVALENT COMPOUNDS AND THEIR PROPERTIES

______**13.** Covalent compounds are formed when a group of atoms share
   a. uncharged particles.   **c.** protons.
   b. neutrons.   **d.** electrons.

______**14.** Compared with ionic bonds, covalent bonds are
   a. weaker.   **c.** larger.
   b. stronger.   **d.** smaller.

______**15.** The group of atoms that make up a covalent compound is called a(n)
   a. bond.   **c.** molecule.
   b. electron.   **d.** atom.

16. What does it mean if a substance is not soluble in water?

____

____

17. Why are covalent compounds often not soluble in water?

____

____

18. Why do covalent compounds have lower melting points than ionic compounds?

____

____

____

Directed Reading A *continued*

19. Why doesn't sugar dissolved in water conduct electric current?

____

____

____

20. How are acids that have been dissolved in water able to conduct an electric current?

____

____

Directed Reading A

Section: Acids and Bases
ACIDS AND THEIR PROPERTIES

_______ **1.** What is any compound that increases the number of hydronium
(H_3O^+) ions dissolved in water called?
   a. base
   b. acid
   c. indicator
   d. neutral

_______ **2.** What does each hydrogen ion bond with to form hydronium ions?
   a. an oxygen particle
   b. a water molecule
   c. an acid
   d. tea

_______ **3.** What do hydrogen ions, H^+, form when they bond to water
molecules, H_2O?
   a. hydrogen ions, H^+
   b. hydronium ions, H_3O^+
   c. water molecules, H_2O
   d. bases

_______ **4.** What flavor do acids have?
   a. sweet
   b. salty
   c. sour
   d. crunchy

_______ **5.** Why should a person NEVER taste or touch an unknown chemical?
   a. many are flavorless
   b. many are too sweet
   c. many are corrosive
   d. many are too salty

_______ **6.** What can corrosive substances destroy?
   a. sour things
   b. poisons
   c. lemons
   d. body tissues and clothing

Directed Reading A *continued*

_______ **7.** A compound that can reversibly change color depending on conditions such as pH is called a(n)
   a. indicator.
   b. color meter.
   c. color changer.
   d. water molecule.

_______ **8.** Two commonly used indicators are bromthymol blue and
   a. hydrochloric acid.
   b. silver nitrate.
   c. litmus paper.
   d. color changer.

_______ **9.** What color does blue litmus paper turn when acid is added to it?
   a. green
   b. red
   c. blue
   d. orange

_______ **10.** What is produced when acids react with some metals?
   a. oxygen gas
   b. metals
   c. silver crystals
   d. hydrogen gas

_______ **11.** Since acids form hydronium ions in water, solutions of acids can
   a. make oxygen.
   b. break apart water molecules.
   c. conduct electric current.
   d. straighten hair.

Match the correct acid with the product it is used in. Write the letter in the space provided.

_______ **12.** rubber

_______ **13.** car batteries

_______ **14.** orange juice

_______ **15.** swimming pools

_______ **16.** soft drinks

a. sulfuric acid

b. nitric acid

c. hydrochloric acid

d. citric acid

e. carbonic acid

| Directed Reading A *continued*

BASES AND THEIR PROPERTIES

_______ **17.** Any compound that increases the number of hydroxide ions when
dissolved in water is a(n)
  a. gas.
  b. sodium.
  c. acid.
  d. base.

_______ **18.** The properties of bases include a bitter taste and a(n)
  a. strong bond.
  b. slippery feel.
  c. hydroxide lattice.
  d. unpleasant odor.

_______ **19.** What should you NEVER do to identify a chemical?
  a. add salt to it
  b. use an indicator
  c. taste or touch
  d. look in a book

_______ **20.** What color does a base change red litmus paper to?
  a. blue
  b. purple
  c. green
  d. orange

_______ **21.** Because bases increase the number of hydroxide ions, OH^-, solutions
of bases can
  a. indicate temperature.
  b. split atoms.
  c. conduct electric current.
  d. stop electric current.

**Match the correct base with the product it is used in. Write the letter in the space
provided.**

_______ **22.** soap

_______ **23.** antacids

_______ **24.** cement

a. magnesium hydroxide

b. sodium hydroxide

c. calcium hydroxide

Directed Reading A

Section: Solutions of Acids and Bases
STRENGTHS OF ACIDS AND BASES

______ 1. What is the amount of acid or base dissolved in water called?
- **a.** concentration
- **b.** strength
- **c.** pH
- **d.** neutralization

______ 2. When an acid or base dissolves in water, what is dependent on the number of molecules that break apart?
- **a.** its concentration
- **b.** its weakness
- **c.** its durability
- **d.** its strength

______ 3. In what kind of solution do all the molecules of an acid break apart in water?
- **a.** a strong acid
- **b.** a strong base
- **c.** a weak acid
- **d.** a weak base

______ 4. In what kind of solution do only a few of the molecules of an acid break apart in water?
- **a.** a strong acid
- **b.** a strong base
- **c.** a weak acid
- **d.** a weak base

______ 5. In what kind of solution do all the molecules of a base break apart?
- **a.** a strong acid
- **b.** a strong base
- **c.** a weak acid
- **d.** a weak base

______ 6. What is a solution called when only a few molecules of a base break apart?
- **a.** a strong acid
- **b.** a strong base
- **c.** a weak acid
- **d.** a weak base

ACIDS, BASES, AND NEUTRALIZATION

______ 7. What is the reaction between acids and bases called?
- **a.** neutralization reaction
- **b.** explosion
- **c.** strength
- **d.** evaporation

______ 8. What do the H^+ ions of an acid and the OH^- ions of a base form when they react?
- **a.** oxygen
- **b.** water
- **c.** sugar
- **d.** hydrogen gas

______ 9. What can show whether a solution contains an acid or a base?
- **a.** an indicator
- **b.** pure water
- **c.** antacids
- **d.** salt

Directed Reading A *continued*

10. A value that is used to express the acidity or basicity (alkalinity) of a system

is called _______________________.

11. The pH of a solution shows the concentration of what type of ion?

____

____

12. What is the pH of a neutral solution?

____

____

13. What type of solution has a pH greater than 7?

____

____

14. What type of solution has a pH less than 7?

____

____

15. What are three examples of common materials with a pH of less than 7?

____

____

____

16. What are three examples of common materials with a pH of more than 7?

____

____

____

For each organism listed, write the preferred pH or pH range.

_______________________ **17.** pine trees

_______________________ **18.** lettuce

_______________________ **19.** fish

Directed Reading A *continued*

20. How does acid rain form, and what is its effect on nature?

____

____

____

SALTS

21. What two substances are produced when an acid neutralizes a base?

____

____

22. What is a salt and how does it form?

____

____

____

23. Name two salts and tell what they are used for.

____

____

____

____

Directed Reading A

Section: Organic Compounds

_______ 1. What is a covalent compound composed of carbon-based molecules
called?
  a. hydrogen atom
  b. oxygen atom
  c. organic compound
  d. valence electron

THE FOUR BONDS OF A CARBON ATOM

_______ 2. How many valence electrons does each carbon atom have?
  a. three
  b. two
  c. six
  d. four

_______ 3. What do structural formulas show about the atoms in a molecule?
  a. what colors the atoms are
  b. how the atoms are connected
  c. how heavy the atoms are
  d. what size the atoms are

_______ 4. What do the backbones of some compounds have hundreds or
thousands of?
  a. carbon atoms
  b. carbon molecules
  c. structural formulas
  d. acid ions

HYDROCARBONS AND OTHER ORGANIC COMPOUNDS

_______ 5. What is an organic compound composed only of carbon and hydrogen
called?
  a. molecule
  b. electron
  c. hydrocarbon
  d. single bond

_______ 6. What is a hydrocarbon in which each carbon atom in the molecule
shares a single bond with each of the four other atoms called?
  a. unsaturated hydrocarbon
  b. saturated hydrocarbon
  c. bonded hydrocarbon
  d. unbonded hydrocarbon

_______ 7. What is another name for a saturated hydrocarbon?
  a. carbon atom
  b. alkane
  c. triple bond
  d. atomic bond

_______ 8. What is a hydrocarbon in which at least one pair of carbon atoms
share a double or triple bond called?
  a. unsaturated hydrocarbon
  b. saturated hydrocarbon
  c. bonded hydrocarbon
  d. unbonded hydrocarbon

Directed Reading A *continued*

______ **9.** What are compounds that contain two carbon atoms connected by a double bond called?

    a. alkanes   **c.** alkenes

    b. double-binds   **d.** alkynes

______ **10.** What are compounds that contain two carbon atoms connected by a triple bond called?

    a. alkanes   **c.** alkenes

    b. triple-binds   **d.** alkynes

11. What are aromatic compounds usually based on?

____

____

12. What kind of bonds do the atoms in a ring of benzene have?

____

____

13. What do aromatic hydrocarbons often have?

____

____

14. List three elements that other organic compounds might have in them.

____

____

BIOCHEMICALS: THE COMPOUNDS OF LIFE

______ **15.** Carbohydrates, lipids, proteins and nucleic acids are the four categories of

    a. living things.   **c.** organic compounds.

    b. unsaturated hydrocarbons.   **d.** biochemicals.

______ **16.** Carbohydrates are biochemicals that are composed of one or more

    a. saturated hydrocarbons.   **c.** organic compounds.

    b. sugar molecules.   **d.** starch molecules.

______ **17.** Carbohydrates are used as a source of

    a. fat.   **c.** energy.

    b. genetic material.   **d.** structure.

______ **18.** Simple carbohydrates are made up of

    a. simple sugars.   **c.** proteins.

    b. cellulose.   **d.** lipids.

| Directed Reading A *continued*

_______**19.** Complex carbohydrates are made of hundreds or thousands of
    a. lipids.
    b. sugar molecules.
    c. proteins.
    d. nucleic acids.

_______**20.** Lipids are biochemicals that do not
    a. store excess energy.
    b. make up cell membranes.
    c. dissolve in water.
    d. store vitamins.

_______**21.** Proteins are biochemicals made up of "building blocks" called
    a. sugars.
    b. amino acids.
    c. nucleic acids.
    d. lipids.

_______**22.** If a single amino acid is missing or out of place, the protein
    a. may not include sulfur.
    b. may not provide support.
    c. may not transport materials.
    d. may not function correctly.

23. List three roles that proteins have in your body and in other living things.

____

____

24. What are the largest molecules made by living organisms called?

____

____

25. What are nucleic acids made up of?

____

____

26. What is the only reason living things differ from each other?

____

____

27. Since nucleic acids contain all the information needed for a cell to make its proteins, what are nucleic acids sometimes called?

____

____

28. What are the two kinds of nucleic acids, and what are their functions?

____

____

Directed Reading B

Section: Ionic and Covalent Compounds

Circle the letter of the best answer for each question.

1. What force of attraction holds atoms together?

a. electrons

b. chemical bond

c. ionic bond

d. valence compounds

2. What kind of electron determines if a compound is covalent or ionic?

a. ionic

b. covalent

c. compound

d. valence

IONIC COMPOUNDS AND THEIR PROPERTIES

Read the words in the box. Read the sentences. Fill in each blank with the word or phrase that best completes the sentence.

ions	metals	ionic compounds

3. An ionic bond is an attraction between oppositely charged

______________________.

4. Compounds that contain ionic bonds are called

______________________.

5. Ionic compounds can be formed when

______________________ react with nonmetals.

Directed Reading B *continued*

Brittleness
Circle the letter of the best answer for each question.

6. What do ionic compounds usually do when they are hit?

   a. roll over

   b. break apart

   c. form a lattice

   d. bond together

7. What kind of structure does an ionic compound have?

   a. ionic

   b. opposite

   c. brittle

   d. crystal lattice

High Melting Points
Read the words in the box. Read the sentences. Fill in each blank with the word that best completes the sentence.

temperatures	ionic

8. Strong bonds make _________________________ compounds

that have high melting points.

9. Ionic compounds melt at higher _________________________

than you could reach in your kitchen.

Solubility and Electrical Conductivity
Circle the letter of the best answer for each question.

10. What do many ionic compounds dissolve in?

   a. air   **c.** oil

   b. water   **d.** current

Directed Reading B *continued*

Circle the letter of the best answer for each question.

11. What do water molecules do to the ions?

   a. push them together

   b. conduct them

   c. pull them apart

   d. heat

12. What can an ionic compound conduct after it dissolves in water?

   a. ions

   b. electric current

   c. crystals

   d. heat

COVALENT COMPOUNDS AND THEIR PROPERTIES

13. Which compound is formed when a group of atoms shares electrons?

   a. ionic compound

   b. properties

   c. covalent compound

   d. ionic bond

14. What is a covalent bond is weaker than?

   a. ionic bond

   b. salt

   c. molecule

   d. properties

Low Solubility

15. What do covalent compounds NOT dissolve well in?

   a. air   **c.** ionic compounds

   b. water   **d.** oils

Directed Reading B *continued*

Low Melting Points

Circle the letter of the best answer for each question.

16. How do the attractive forces of covalent compounds differ from those of ionic compounds?

   a. weaker   **c.** larger

   b. stronger   **d.** smaller

17. Which of the following compounds has a lower melting point than an ionic compound?

   a. covalent compound

   b. salt compound

   c. soluble compound

   d. water compound

Electrical Conductivity

18. What do very few covalent compounds dissolve in?

   a. ionic compounds

   b. solutions of sugar

   c. water

   d. sugar

19. What kind of compounds are many acids?

   a. attractive

   b. covalent

   c. ionic

   d. molecules

20. What can ionic compounds do that some covalent compounds like sugar can't?

   a. make sugar

   b. get rid of ions

   c. conduct electric current

   d. find solutions

Directed Reading B

Section: Acids and Bases

ACIDS AND THEIR PROPERTIES

Circle the letter of the best answer for each question.

1. What is a compound that increases hydronium ions in solution called?

   a. oxygen

   b. acid

   c. indicator

   d. carbon

2. What kind of ions separate from acids in solution?

   a. oxygen   **c.** water

   b. carbon   **d.** hydrogen

3. What do hydrogen ions usually bond with?

   a. oxygen   **c.** water

   b. carbon   **d.** hydrogen

Acids Have a Sour Flavor

Read the words in the box. Read the sentences. Fill in each blank with the word that best completes the sentence.

corrosive	acids	citric

4. Foods that taste sour usually contain

   ___________________________.

5. The taste of citrus fruits comes from

   ___________________________ acid.

6. Many acids are ___________________________.

| Directed Reading B *continued*

Acids Change Colors in Indicators
Circle the letter of the best answer for each question.

7. What is a compound that can change color depending on conditions such as the pH?

a. water

b. hydrogen

c. litmus

d. indicator

8. What happens when acid is added to blue litmus paper?

a. the paper turns red

b. the paper turns green

c. the paper stays blue

d. the paper turns orange

Acids React With Metals

9. What do acids that react with some metals produce?

a. oxygen gas

b. hydrogen gas

c. natural gas

d. helium gas

Acids Conduct Electric Current

10. Because acids form ions, what can they conduct?

a. water molecules

b. acid solutions

c. electric current

d. hydronium

Directed Reading B *continued*

Uses of Acids

Read the description. Then, <u>draw a line</u> from the dot next to each description to the matching word.

11. used in car batteries ●   **a.** hydrochloric acid

12. used in plastics ●   **b.** nitric acid

13. used in soft drinks ●   **c.** sulfuric acid

14. used in swimming pools ●   **d.** carbonic acid

BASES AND THEIR PROPERTIES

<u>Circle the letter</u> of the best answer for each question.

15. What is a compound that adds hydroxide ions when dissolved in water called?

   a. an acid

   b. a base

   c. sodium

   d. neutral

Bases Have a Bitter Flavor and a Slippery Feel

16. What gives soap a bitter taste and slippery feel?

   a. a base

   b. an acid

   c. dirt

   d. water

17. Why should you NEVER taste or touch an unknown base?

   a. many are slimy

   b. many are too watery

   c. many turn colors

   d. many are corrosive

| Directed Reading B *continued*

Bases Change Color in Indicators

Circle the letter of the best answer for each question.

18. Bases change the color of red litmus paper to what color?

a. green

b. blue

c. orange

d. pink

Bases Conduct Electric Current

19. Because bases increase hydroxide ions in solution, what can they conduct?

a. water molecules

b. negativity

c. hydrogen

d. electric current

Uses of Bases

Read the description. Then, draw a line from the dot next to each description to the matching word.

20. used in soap ● **a.** ammonia

21. used in cement ● **b.** calcium hydroxide

22. used in antacids ● **c.** magnesium hydroxide

23. used in household cleaners ● **d.** sodium hydroxide

Skills Worksheet

Directed Reading B

Section: Solutions of Acids and Bases
STRENGTHS OF ACIDS AND BASES

Circle the letter of the best answer for each question.

1. What does the strength of an acid or base depend on?

   a. molecules that bond together

   b. concentrations

   c. molecules that break apart

   d. the amount of the acids or base

Strong Versus Weak Acids

2. When a strong acid dissolves in water, how many molecules break apart?

   a. only a few

   b. about a fourth

   c. about half

   d. all

3. When a weak acid dissolves in water, how many molecules break apart?

   a. only a few

   b. about a fourth

   c. about half

   d. all

Strong Versus Weak Bases

4. How would you describe a base if all the molecules of the base break apart the water?

   a. weak base

   b. neutral

   c. strong base

   d. medium strong base

| Directed Reading B *continued*

ACIDS, BASES, AND NEUTRALIZATION

Read the words in the box. Read the sentences. <u>Fill in each blank</u> with the word that best completes the sentence.

salt	neutralization	water

5. When acids and bases combine, it is called a

_______________________________ reaction.

6. H^+ ions in an acid and OH^- ions in a base combine to

form _______________________________.

7. If the water in an acid-base solution evaporates, the ions form a

_______________________________.

The pH Scale

<u>Circle the letter</u> of the best answer for each question.

8. What is the value used to express acidity or alkalinity called?

   a. solution

   b. indicator

   c. pH

   d. concentration

9. What shows if a solution has an acid or a base?

   a. water

   b. indicator

   c. electric current

   d. concentrations

Directed Reading B *continued*

Circle the letter of the best answer for each question.

10. What is the pH of a neutral solution such as pure water?

  a. 7

  b. 4

  c. 1

  d. 9

11. What is the pH of a basic solution?

  a. less than 7

  b. greater than 7

  c. 7

  d. 3

12. What is the pH of an acidic solution?

  a. greater than 7

  b. less than 7

  c. 7

  d. 3

Read the description. Then, draw a line from the dot next to each solution to the matching substance.

13. basic solution ● **a.** lemon juice

14. acidic solution ● **b.** detergent

15. neutral solution ● **c.** pure water

❚ Directed Reading B *continued*

Using Indicators to Determine pH
Circle the letter of the best answer for each question.

16. What is used to determine whether a solution contains an acid or base?

  a. concentration

  b. solution

  c. measurement

  d. single indicator

17. What can a group of indicators be used to find?

  a. paper strips

  b. pH

  c. pH meter

  d. concentration

pH and the Environment

18. What do living things need in their environment?

  a. electron

  b. a certain pH

  c. color

  d. indicator

19. What can die if acid rain lowers the pH of lakes?

  a. indicators

  b. robins

  c. fish

  d. rocks

SALTS

20. What is formed when an acid neutralizes a base?

  a. water and a salt

  b. snow and ice

  c. a chemical

  d. a high pH

Uses of Salts

Three different substances are listed below. Draw a line from the dot next to each substance to the matching compound.

21. food preservative   ●   **a.** sodium chloride

22. lye   ●   **b.** sodium hydroxide

23. food seasoning   ●   **c.** sodium nitrate

Directed Reading B

Section: Organic Compounds

<u>Circle the letter</u> of the best answer for each question.

1. What are covalent compounds made of carbon-based molecules called?

   a. organic compounds

   b. sulfuric compounds

   c. ionic compounds

   d. fuel compounds

2. What are organic compounds made of?

   a. metals

   b. water molecules

   c. carbon-based molecules

   d. acids

THE FOUR BONDS OF A CARBON ATOM

3. What can each carbon atom can make four bonds with?

   a. four other molecules

   b. three other atoms

   c. four other atoms

   d. two sugars

Carbon Backbones

4. What do structural formulas show about atoms in a molecule?

   a. what color the atoms are

   b. what size the atoms are

   c. how heavy the atoms are

   d. how atoms are connected

HYDROCARBONS AND OTHER ORGANIC COMPOUNDS

5. What is an organic compound that contains only carbon and hydrogen called?

   a. alkyne

   b. oxygen compound

   c. covalent compound

   d. hydrocarbon

| Directed Reading B *continued*

Saturated Hydrocarbons

<u>Circle the letter</u> of the best answer for each question.

6. In a saturated hydrocarbon, how many atoms does each carbon atom bond with?

   a. two   **c.** four

   b. three   **d.** one

7. What is the other name for a saturated hydrocarbon?

   a. alkane   **c.** single-bond carbon

   b. alkene   **d.** alkyne

Unsaturated Hydrocarbons

Read the words in the box. Read the sentences. <u>Fill in each blank</u> with the word or phrase that best completes the sentence.

alkenes	unsaturated
alkynes	electrons

8. A hydrocarbon that is ___________________________ has one pair

of that share a double or triple bond.

9. A double bond is made up of two pairs of

shared _______________________.

10. Hydrocarbons with double bonds are called

_______________________.

11. Hydrocarbons with triple bonds are called

_______________________.

Aromatic Hydrocarbons

<u>Circle the letter</u> of the best answer for the question.

12. What are most aromatic hydrocarbons based on?

   a. propane   **c.** ethene

   b. benzene   **d.** ethyne

| Directed Reading B *continued*

Circle the letter of the best answer for each question.

13. What kind of odor (or smell) do aromatic compounds have?

    a. almost odorless   **c.** strong

    b. bad   **d.** weak

Other Organic Compounds

14. What organic compound has a straight chain structure?

    a. glycogen   **c.** sulfur

    b. glucose   **d.** cellulose

BIOCHEMICALS: THE COMPOUNDS OF LIFE

15. What are organic compounds made by living things called?

    a. living organics   **c.** biochemicals

    b. organic chemicals   **d.** carbohydrate chemicals

Carbohydrates

Read the words in the box. Read the sentences. Fill in each blank with the word or phrase that best completes the sentence.

simple	carbohydrates
complex	plants

16. A class of nutrients that includes sugar, starches, and fiber is

called ____________________________.

17. Carbohydrates also provide the main structure

of ____________________________.

18. Sugars like glucose make up ____________________________

carbohydrates.

19. Hundreds and thousands of sugar molecules can

make ____________________________ carbohydrates.

Directed Reading B *continued*

Lipids

Circle the letter of the best answer for each question.

20. What type of biochemical does not dissolve in water?

    a. protein

    b. lipid

    c. carbohydrate

    d. vitamin

21. What do lipids store?

    a. energy

    b. starch

    c. plants

    d. vitamins

Proteins

Read the words in the box. Read the sentences. Fill in each blank with the word or phrase that best completes the sentence.

sulfur	amino acids	proteins

22. Biochemicals made up of amino acids are called

_______________________________.

23. Molecules made up of carbon, hydrogen, oxygen and nitrogen

atoms are called _______________________________.

24. Some amino acids also include _______________________________

atoms.

Directed Reading B *continued*

Examples of Proteins

Read the words in the box. Read the sentences. <u>Fill in each blank</u> with the word or phrase that best completes the sentence.

nucleotides	hemoglobin
nucleic acids	catalysts

25. Enzymes are proteins that are _______________________.

26. A protein called _______________________ is found in red

blood cells.

Nucleic Acids

27. The largest molecules made by living things are

_______________________.

28. Molecules made of carbon, hydrogen, oxygen, nitrogen, and

phosphorus atoms are called _______________________.

DNA and RNA

Read the description. Then, <u>draw a line</u> from the dot next to each description to the matching word.

29. make up the DNA ladder   ●   **a.** DNA

30. helps build proteins   ●   **b.** RNA

31. a cell's genetic material   ●   **c.** nucleotides

Name _______________________ Class _______________ Date _______________

Vocabulary and Section Summary

Ionic and Covalent Compounds

VOCABULARY

In your own words, write a definition of the following terms in the space provided.

1. chemical bond

2. ionic compound

3. covalent compound

SECTION SUMMARY

Read the following section summary.

- Ionic compounds have ionic bonds between ions of opposite charges.
- Ionic compounds are usually brittle, have high melting points, dissolve in water, and often conduct an electric current.
- Covalent compounds have covalent bonds and consist of particles called *molecules*.
- Covalent compounds have low melting points, don't dissolve easily in water, and do not conduct electric current.

Vocabulary and Section Summary

Acids and Bases

VOCABULARY

In your own words, write a definition of the following terms in the space provided.

1. acid

____

____

2. indicator

____

____

3. base

____

____

SECTION SUMMARY

Read the following section summary.

- An acid is a compound that increases the number of hydronium ions in solution.
- Acids taste sour, turn blue litmus paper red, react with metals to produce hydrogen gas, and may conduct an electric current when in solution.
- Acids are used for industrial purposes and in household products.
- A base is a compound that increases the number of hydroxide ions in solution.
- Bases taste bitter, feel slippery, and turn red litmus paper blue. Most solutions of bases conduct an electric current.
- Bases are used in cleaning products and acid neutralizers.

Vocabulary and Section Summary

Solutions of Acids and Bases

VOCABULARY

In your own words, write a definition of the following terms in the space provided.

1. neutralization reaction

____

____

2. pH

____

____

3. salt

____

____

SECTION SUMMARY

Read the following section summary.

- Every molecule of a strong acid or base breaks apart to form ions. Few molecules of weak acids and bases break apart to form ions.

- An acid and a base can neutralize one another to make salt and water.

- pH is a measure of hydronium ion concentration in a solution.

- A salt is an ionic compound formed in a neutralization reaction. Salts have many industrial and household uses.

Skills Worksheet

Vocabulary and Section Summary

Organic Compounds
VOCABULARY

In your own words, write a definition of the following terms in the space provided.

1. organic compound

____

____

2. hydrocarbon

____

____

3. carbohydrate

____

____

4. lipid

____

____

5. protein

____

____

6. nucleic acid

____

____

Vocabulary and Section Summary *continued*

SECTION SUMMARY

Read the following section summary.

- Organic compounds contain carbon, which can form four bonds.
- Hydrocarbons are composed of only carbon and hydrogen.
- Hydrocarbons may be saturated, unsaturated, or aromatic hydrocarbons.
- Carbohydrates are made of simple sugars.
- Lipids store energy and make up cell membranes.
- Proteins are composed of amino acids.
- Nucleic acids store genetic information and help cells make protein.

Section Review

Ionic and Covalent Compounds

USING KEY TERMS

1. Use each of the following terms in a separate sentence: *ionic compound,* *covalent compound,* and *chemical bond.*

____

____

____

UNDERSTANDING KEY IDEAS

______ 2. Which of the following describes an ionic compound?
   - **a.** It has a low melting point.
   - **b.** It consists of shared electrons.
   - **c.** It conducts electric current in water solutions.
   - **d.** It consists of two nonmetals.

3. List two properties of covalent compounds.

____

____

MATH SKILLS

4. A compound contains 39.37% chromium, 38.10% oxygen, and potassium. What percentage of the compound is potassium? Show your work below.

Section Review *continued*

CRITICAL THINKING

5. Making Inferences Solid crystals of ionic compounds do not conduct an electric current. But when the crystals dissolve in water, the solution conducts an electric current. Explain.

____

____

____

____

6. Applying Concepts Some white solid crystals are dissolved in water. If the solution does not conduct an electric current, is the solid an ionic compound or a covalent compound? Explain.

____

____

____

____

Section Review

Acids and Bases

USING KEY TERMS

1. In your own words, write a definition for each of the following terms: *acid,* *base,* and *indicator.*

____

____

____

UNDERSTANDING KEY IDEAS

_______ **2.** A base is a substance that
    a. feels slippery.
    b. tastes sour.
    c. reacts with metals to produce hydrogen gas.
    d. turns blue litmus paper red.

_______ **3.** Acids are important in
    a. making antacids.
    b. preparing detergents.
    c. keeping algae out of swimming pools.
    d. manufacturing cement.

4. What happens to red litmus paper when it touches a base?

____

____

MATH SKILLS

5. A cake recipe calls for 472 mL of milk. You don't have a metric measuring cup at home, so you need to convert milliliters to cups. You know that 1 L equals 1.06 quarts and that there are 4 cups in 1 quart. How many cups of milk will you need to use? Show your work below.

| Section Review *continued*

CRITICAL THINKING

6. Making Comparisons Compare the properties of acids and bases.

____

____

____

____

7. Applying Concepts Why would it be useful for a gardener or a vegetable farmer to use litmus paper to test soil samples?

____

____

____

____

8. Analyzing Processes Suppose that your teacher gives you a solution of an unknown chemical. The chemical is either an acid or a base. You know that touching or tasting acids and bases is not safe. What two tests could you perform on the chemical to determine whether it is an acid or a base? What results would help you decide if the chemical was an acid or a base?

____

____

____

____

Name _________________________________ Class _______________ Date ____________

Section Review

Solutions of Acids and Bases

USING KEY TERMS

1. Use the following terms in the same sentence: *neutralization reaction* and *salt*.

____

____

UNDERSTANDING KEY IDEAS

_______ 2. A neutralization reaction
   a. includes an acid and a base.
   b. produces a salt.
   c. forms water.
   d. All of the above

3. Explain the difference between a strong acid and a weak acid.

____

____

MATH SKILLS

4. For each point lower on the pH scale, the hydrogen ions in solution increase tenfold. For example, a solution of pH 3 is not twice as acidic as a solution of pH 6 but is 1,000 times as acidic. How many times more acidic is a solution of pH 2 than a solution of pH 4? Show your work below.

❙ Section Review *continued*

CRITICAL THINKING

5. Analyzing Processes Predict what will happen to the hydrogen ion concentration and the pH of water if hydrochloric acid is added to the water.

____

____

____

____

6. Analyzing Relationships Would fish be healthy in a lake that has a low pH? Explain.

____

____

____

____

7. Applying Concepts Soap is made from a strong base and oil. Would you expect the pH of soap to be 4 or 9? Explain.

____

____

____

____

Section Review

Organic Compounds

USING KEY TERMS

1. Use the following terms in the same sentence: *organic compound,*
hydrocarbon, and *biochemical.*

2. In your own words, write a definition for each of the following terms:
carbohydrate, lipid, protein, and *nucleic acid.*

UNDERSTANDING KEY IDEAS

______ **3.** A saturated hydrocarbon has
   a. only single bonds.
   b. double bonds.
   c. triple bonds.
   d. double and triple bonds.

4. List two functions of proteins.

Section Review *continued*

5. What is an aromatic hydrocarbon?

____

____

CRITICAL THINKING

6. Identifying Relationships Hemoglobin is a protein that is in blood and that transports oxygen to the tissues of the body. Information stored in nucleic acids tells a cell how to make proteins. What might happen if there is a mistake in the information needed to make hemoglobin?

____

____

____

7. Making Comparisons Compare saturated hydrocarbons with unsaturated hydrocarbons.

____

____

____

INTERPRETING GRAPHICS

Use the structural formula of this organic compound to answer the following questions.

$$
\begin{array}{ccccccc}
 & H & & H & & H & \\
 & | & & | & & | & \\
H- & C & - & C & - & C & -H \\
 & | & & | & & | & \\
 & H & & H & & H & \\
\end{array}
$$

8. What type of bonds are present in this molecule?

____

____

9. Can you determine the shape of the molecule from this structural formula? Explain your answer.

____

____

Chapter Review

USING KEY TERMS

For each pair of terms, explain how the meanings of the terms differ.

1. *ionic compound* and *covalent compound*

2. *acid* and *base*

3. *pH* and *indicator*

4. *hydrocarbon* and *organic compound*

5. *carbohydrate* and *lipid*

6. *protein* and *nucleic acid*

UNDERSTANDING KEY IDEAS

Multiple Choice

_______ 7. Which of the following statements describes lipids?
   a. Lipids are used to store energy.
   b. Lipids do not dissolve in water.
   c. Lipids make up part of the cell membrane.
   d. All of the above

▌Chapter Review *continued*

_______ **8.** Ionic compounds
    a. have a low melting point.
    b. are often brittle.
    c. do not conduct electric current in water.
    d. do not dissolve easily in water.

_______ **9.** An increase in the concentration of hydronium ions in solution
    a. raises the pH.   **c.** does not affect the pH.
    b. lowers the pH.   **d.** doubles the pH.

_______ **10.** The compounds that store information for building proteins are
    a. lipids.   **c.** nucleic acids.
    b. hydrocarbons.   **d.** carbohydrates.

SHORT ANSWER

11. What type of compound would you use to neutralize a solution of potassium hydroxide?

____

12. Explain why the reaction of an acid with a base is called *neutralization.*

____

____

13. What characteristic of carbon atoms helps to explain the wide variety of organic compounds?

____

____

14. What kind of ions are produced when an acid is dissolved in water and when a base is dissolved in water?

____

MATH SKILLS

15. Most of the vinegar used to make pickles is 5% acetic acid. So, in 100 mL of vinegar, 5 mL is acid diluted with 95 mL of water. If you bought a 473 mL bottle of 5% vinegar, how many milliliters of acetic acid would be in the bottle? How many milliliters of water were used to dilute the acetic acid? Show your work below.

Chapter Review *continued*

---

16. If you dilute a 75 mL can of orange juice with enough water to make a total volume of 300 mL, what is the percentage of juice in the mixture? Show your work below.

CRITICAL THINKING

17. Concept Mapping Use the following terms to create a concept map: *acid, base, salt, neutral,* and *pH*.

Chapter Review *continued*

---

18. Applying Concepts Fish give off the base, ammonia, NH_3, as waste. How does the release of ammonia affect the pH of the water in the aquarium? What can be done to correct the pH of the water?

____

____

____

19. Analyzing Methods Many insects, such as fire ants, inject formic acid, a weak acid, when they bite or sting. Describe the type of compound that should be used to treat the bite.

____

____

____

____

20. Making Comparisons Organic compounds are also covalent compounds. What properties would you expect organic compounds to have as a result?

____

____

____

____

21. Applying Concepts Farmers have been known to taste their soil to determine whether the soil has the correct acidity for their plants. How would taste help the farmer determine the acidity of the soil?

____

____

____

| Chapter Review *continued*

22. Analyzing Ideas A diet that includes a high level of lipids is unhealthy. Why is a diet containing no lipids also unhealthy?

____

____

____

INTERPRETING GRAPHICS

Use the structural formulas below to answer the questions that follow.

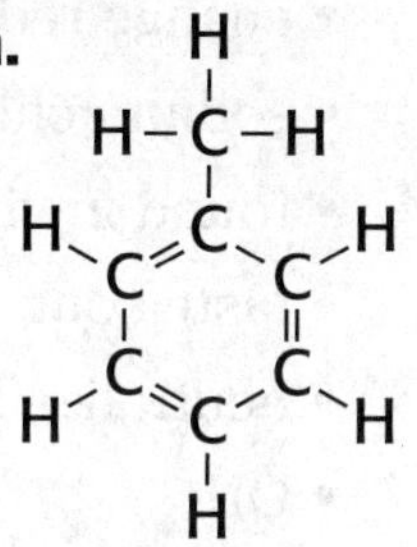

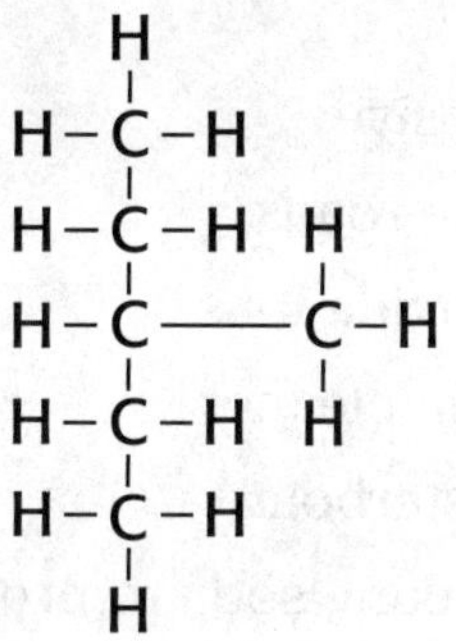

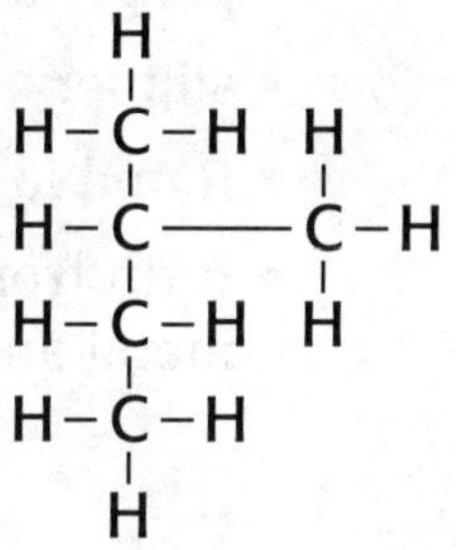

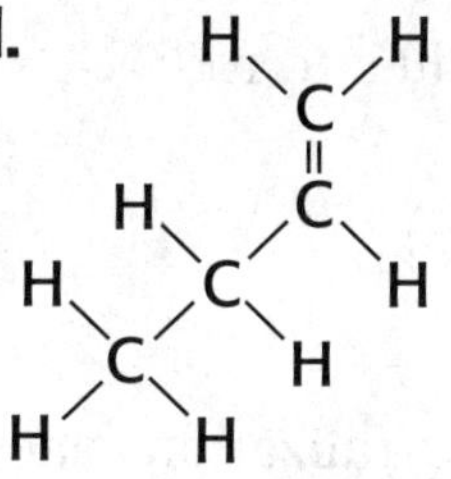

23. A saturated hydrocarbon is represented by which structural formula(s)?

____

24. An unsaturated hydrocarbon is represented by which structural formula(s)?

____

25. An aromatic hydrocarbon is represented by which structural formula(s)?

____

Reinforcement

A Simple Solution

Complete this worksheet after you finish reading the section "Solutions of Acids and Bases."

Libby Lidmis has been busy gathering information on acids, bases, and salts. Unfortunately, someone mixed up the information on her chart. Each of the pieces of information given below describes an acid, a base, or a salt. Help Libby straighten out her chart by matching each piece of information with the correct categories, and writing it in the appropriate box on the next page. Be careful—some of the pieces of information belong in more than one category.

- taste bitter
- may be corrosive
- used to de-ice roads
- excess hydroxide ions
- found in drain cleaner
- found in plasterboard
- react with baking soda to produce carbon dioxide gas
- change blue litmus to red
- pH less than 7
- used to make soap
- H^+
- form from a neutralization reaction

- change red litmus to blue
- sodium chloride
- found in vinegar
- taste sour
- neutralize lakes with low pH
- OH^-
- excess hydronium ions
- pH greater than 7
- slippery
- found in orange juice
- form from the reaction of a metal and a nonmetal

Reinforcement *continued*

<table>
<tr><td align="center">ACIDS</td></tr>
<tr><td>

</td></tr>
</table>

<table>
<tr><td align="center">BASES</td></tr>
<tr><td>

</td></tr>
</table>

<table>
<tr><td align="center">SALTS</td></tr>
<tr><td>

</td></tr>
</table>

Critical Thinking

Battle of the Breads

Host: Last week on Culinary Challenge, we had two popular bakery chefs as our guests, Bess Season and Phil R. Roma. Bess is known for the fluffy texture of her wheat bread, while Phil is known for the flavor of his soda bread. Let's hear a quick recap of last week's heated debate:

Chef Season: I begin by mixing flour, water, and yeast. The yeast produce carbon dioxide bubbles. The flour and water form elastic sheets that trap and hold the carbon dioxide bubbles. Within a few hours, my mouth-watering wheat bread . . .

Chef Roma: No one wants to wait hours for bread to rise! I can make my bread in less than an hour by using baking soda and cream of tartar instead of yeast. It is quick, convenient, and when you bite into . . .

Chef Season: When you bite into soda bread, it is as flat as a pancake!

Host: During the contest, each chef made small changes to his or her recipe. Chef Season added butter for richer flavor. Chef Roma added extra cream of tartar to help his bread rise. Who baked the fluffiest, tastiest loaf of bread? Stay tuned.

USEFUL TERMS
culinary related to cooking
yeast a fungus that feeds on carbohydrates and produces alcohol and carbon dioxide

ANALYZING IDEAS

1. Why does Chef Season's wheat bread rise?

____

____

____

____

Critical Thinking *continued*

2. Why does Chef Roma's soda bread rise?

HELPFUL HINT
Cream of tartar is an acid.

____

____

____

____

____

PREDICTING CONSEQUENCES

3. a. Chef Season begins by mixing butter with flour. Then she adds water to the mixture. How will this change the way the ingredients combine?

HELPFUL HINT
Butter is a covalent compound.

____

____

____

b. How will mixing butter with flour and then adding water affect the fluffiness of Chef Season's bread?

____

____

____

4. What might happen to the flavor of Chef Roma's bread when he adds extra cream of tartar?

____

____

____

| Critical Thinking *continued*

DRAWING CONCLUSIONS

5. Who do you think will win the culinary challenge? Explain.

____

____

____

____

____

Assessment

Section Quiz

Section: Ionic and Covalent Compounds

Match the correct description with the correct term. Write the letter in the space provided.

_______ **1.** the force of attraction that holds atoms or ions together

_______ **2.** compound made of oppositely charged ions

_______ **3.** located in the outermost energy level of an atom; their behavior determines what kind of compound is formed

_______ **4.** a chemical compound formed by the sharing of electrons

a. covalent compound

b. chemical bond

c. ionic compound

d. valence electrons

Write the letter of the correct answer in the space provided.

_______ **5.** If it is brittle, dissolves easily in water, has a high melting point and conducts electric current it is a(n)
   a. valence electron.   **c.** covalent compound.
   b. ionic compound.   **d.** sugar.

_______ **6.** Which compound has the weaker chemical bond?
   a. ionic   **c.** metallic
   b. covalent   **d.** electric

_______ **7.** When a metal reacts with a nonmetal it makes
   a. an ionic compound.   **c.** a low melting point.
   b. a covalent compound.   **d.** water molecules.

_______ **8.** Most covalent compounds
   a. dissolve in water.   **c.** mix with water.
   b. don't dissolve in water.   **d.** are positively charged in water.

_______ **9.** Sugar is a covalent compound that dissolves in water but does not form ions, so it
   a. conducts electric current.
   b. does not conduct electric current.
   c. is negatively charged.
   d. is not a compound.

_______ **10.** Covalent compounds have
   a. high melting points.   **c.** no melting point.
   b. low melting points.   **d.** strong bonds.

Name _________________________________ Class _______________ Date ____________

Section Quiz

Section: Acids and Bases

Match the correct description with the correct term. Write the letter in the space provided.

______ **1.** any compound that increases the number of hydronium ions when dissolved in water

______ **2.** a compound that can reversibly change color depending on conditions such as pH

______ **3.** any compound that increases the number of hydroxide ions when dissolved in water

a. indicator

b. base

c. acid

Write the letter of the correct answer in the space provided.

______ **4.** What substances can acids react with to produce hydrogen gas?
　　a. water　　　　　**c.** metals
　　b. sugars　　　　 **d.** poisons

______ **5.** Acids conduct electric current by forming
　　a. hydrochloric acids.　　**c.** hydronium ions.
　　b. hydrogen gases.　　　 **d.** hydroxide ions.

______ **6.** Acids have a
　　a. sour taste.　　　**c.** slippery feel.
　　b. bitter taste.　　 **d.** soapy feel.

______ **7.** Bases have a
　　a. sour taste.　　　**c.** slippery feel.
　　b. sweet taste.　　 **d.** mild taste.

______ **8.** When a base is added to red litmus paper, the indicator turns
　　a. blue.　　　**c.** purple.
　　b. red.　　　 **d.** orange.

______ **9.** If a cleaning product includes ammonia as an ingredient, it probably is made from a(n)
　　a. acid.　　　**c.** indicator.
　　b. base.　　　**d.** powder.

Section Quiz

Section: Solutions of Acids and Bases

Match the correct description with the correct term. Write the letter in the space provided.

_______ **1.** a value used to express the acidity or alkalinity (basicity) of a system

_______ **2.** an ionic compound formed from the positive ion of a base and the negative ion of an acid when they combine

_______ **3.** the reaction of an acid and a base to form a neutral solution of water and a salt

_______ **4.** measured by pH

a. neutralization reaction

b. hydronium ion concentration

c. pH

d. salt

Write the letter of the correct answer in the space provided.

_______ **5.** When all the molecules of an acid break apart in water, the solution is called a
  a. weak acid.
  b. strong acid.
  c. weak base.
  d. strong base.

_______ **6.** Citric acid is a weak acid, so only a few molecules would break apart when
  a. it comes in contact with air.
  b. it dissolves in water.
  c. it neutralizes.
  d. it is forming.

_______ **7.** When acids and bases come in contact with each other, they
  a. explode.
  b. become bitter.
  c. make hydroxide.
  d. neutralize each other.

_______ **8.** One way to test pH is to use a strip of paper that has several
  a. hydronium ions.
  b. bases.
  c. acids.
  d. indicators.

_______ **9.** A neutral solution has a pH of
  a. 7.
  b. 11.
  c. 3.
  d. 1.

_______ **10.** Sodium chloride, sodium nitrate and calcium sulfate are all
  a. sugars.
  b. hydroniums.
  c. indicators.
  d. salts.

Assessment

Section Quiz

Section: Organic Compounds

Match the correct description with the correct term. Write the letter in the space provided.

______ **1.** a covalently bonded compound that has carbon-based molecules

______ **2.** an organic compound composed only of carbon and hydrogen

______ **3.** a class of energy-giving nutrients that includes sugars, starches and fiber

______ **4.** a type of biochemical that does not dissolve in water, includes fats and steroids

______ **5.** an organic compound that is made of one or more chains of amino acids and is in all cells

______ **6.** an organic compound, either RNA or DNA, whose molecules are made up of one or two chains of nucleotides

a. nucleic acid

b. protein

c. carbohydrate

d. organic compound

e. hydrocarbon

f. lipid

Write the letter of the correct answer in the space provided.

______ **7.** How many atoms can a carbon atom make bonds with?
- **a.** one
- **b.** two
- **c.** three
- **d.** four

______ **8.** Which hydrocarbon contains only single bonds between carbon atoms?
- **a.** saturated
- **b.** unsaturated
- **c.** aromatic
- **d.** inorganic

______ **9.** Carbohydrates, lipids, proteins, and nucleic acids are all
- **a.** hydrocarbons
- **b.** biochemicals
- **c.** fats
- **d.** plants

______ **10.** What are aromatic hydrocarbons based on?
- **a.** water
- **b.** alkenes
- **c.** benzene
- **d.** lipids

Name _________________________________ Class ______________ Date ____________

Chemical Compounds
MULTIPLE CHOICE
Write the letter of the correct answer in the space provided.

_______ **1.** Brittleness and a high melting point are two properties of
 a. covalent compounds.
 b. organic compounds.
 c. ionic compounds.
 d. protein compounds.

_______ **2.** What kind of compound rarely dissolves in water?
 a. ionic
 b. organic
 c. protein
 d. covalent

_______ **3.** What substance has a sour taste and produces hydrogen gas when it
 reacts with some metals?
 a. base
 b. organic compound
 c. acid
 d. indicator

_______ **4.** This substance has a bitter taste and slippery feel.
 a. base
 b. organic compound
 c. acid
 d. indicator

_______ **5.** If almost all the molecules of an acid break apart when dissolved in
 water, the acid is
 a. weak.
 b. neutral.
 c. strong.
 d. sour.

_______ **6.** A substance that is rated 7 on the pH scale is considered
 a. basic.
 b. neutral.
 c. weak.
 d. acidic.

Name ___________________________________ Class _______________ Date ___________

_______ **7.** When an acid and a base neutralize each other, what remains?
   a. a weak acid and base
   b. a strong acid and base
   c. water and a salt.
   d. a lipid and a protein

_______ **8.** Over 90% of compounds are what type?
   a. ionic
   b. organic
   c. inorganic
   d. covalent

_______ **9.** What type of hydrocarbon has double and triple bonds between carbon atoms?
   a. saturated
   b. aromatic
   c. unsaturated
   d. neutral

_______ **10.** Biochemicals composed of one or more simple sugar molecules are called
   a. proteins.
   b. nucleic acids.
   c. lipids.
   d. carbohydrates.

MATCHING

Match the correct definition with the correct term. Write the letter in the space provided.

_______**11.** a chemical compound formed by the sharing of electrons

_______**12.** an ionic compound formed from the positive ion of a base and the negative ion of an acid

_______**13.** the force of attraction that holds atoms or ions together

_______**14.** a type of biochemical that does not dissolve in water

_______**15.** an organic compound that contains only carbon and hydrogen

_______**16.** a compound that can change color depending on the pH of the solution

_______**17.** an organic compound that carries genetic information

_______**18.** a value that is used to express the acidity or basicity (alkalinity) of a system

a. hydrocarbon

b. chemical bond

c. indicator

d. salt

e. pH

f. lipid

g. covalent compound

h. nucleic acid

Chapter Test A *continued*

MATCHING

Match the correct description with the correct term. Write the letter in the space provided.

_______**19.** composed of amino acids

_______**20.** include fats, oils and waves

_______**21.** include sugars, starches and fiber

_______**22.** sometimes called the blueprints of life

a. carbohydrates

b. lipids

c. proteins

d. nucleic acids

Match the correct description with the correct term. Write the letter in the space provided.

_______**23.** may kill fish and other organisms

_______**24.** used to preserve food

_______**25.** occurs when acids and bases react

a. neutralization reaction

b. acid rain

c. sodium nitrate

Chapter Test B

Chemical Compounds

USING KEY TERMS

Use the terms from the following list to complete the sentences below. Each term may be used only once. Some terms may not be used.

proteins   base   ionic
nucleic acid   salt   covalent

1. When electrons are shared between atoms of two different elements

_______________________ compounds are formed.

2. Limewater with a pH of 10.5 is a(n) _______________________.

3. Enzymes are _______________________ that increase the rate of chemical

reactions in biological systems.

4. When an acid neutralizes a base, a(n) _______________________ is formed.

5. RNA is a(n) _______________________ that plays an active role in

protein synthesis.

UNDERSTANDING KEY IDEAS

Write the letter of the correct answer in the space provided.

_______ **6.** Hemoglobin, which carries oxygen in the blood, is a
     a. carbohydrate.   **c.** protein.
     b. lipid.   **d.** nucleic acid.

_______ **7.** Which of the following make up over 90% of all known compounds?
     a. ionic compounds   **c.** basic compounds
     b. organic compounds   **d.** aromatic compounds

_______ **8.** Vitamins that do not dissolve in water are stored in
     a. lipids.   **c.** carbohydrates.
     b. proteins.   **d.** nucleic acids.

_______ **9.** The walls of cell membranes are made of what kind of biochemical?
     a. protein   **c.** cholesterol
     b. cellulose   **d.** lipid

| Chapter Test B *continued*

______10. Glucose is a
    a. wax.
    b. starch
    c. simple carbohydrate.
    d. complex carbohydrate.

______11. Which of the following, in equal concentrations, has the lowest pH?
    a. salt
    b. strong base
    c. strong acid
    d. a weak acid

______12. Which of these statements about proteins is incorrect?
    a. Certain proteins provide structural support for cells.
    b. Proteins are involved in the transport of molecules across membranes.
    c. The function of a protein depends on its shape.
    d. Nucleic acids are the building blocks of proteins.

______13. Which of the following is an ionic compound?
    a. glucose
    b. water
    c. sodium chloride
    d. vegetable oil

14. In what ways do changes in pH affect the environment and living things?

____

____

____

____

____

15. How are ionic compounds different from covalent compounds?

____

____

____

____

____

16. Describe the main difference between simple and complex carbohydrates.

____

____

____

CRITICAL THINKING

17. How could a spill-response team use neutralization to safely clean up a large spill of hydrochloric acid?

____

____

____

____

____

18. A student added a few drops of lemon juice to a glass of red cabbage juice. The lemon juice turned the cabbage juice pink. When the student added a few drops of liquid soap to the red cabbage juice, the juice turned green. What function did the red cabbage juice serve? Explain.

____

____

____

____

____

19. Many insects, such as fire ants, inject formic acid, a weak acid, when they bite or sting. What kind of compound should be used to treat this kind of bite?

____

____

____

____

____

Chapter Test B *continued*

CONCEPT MAPPING

20. Use the following terms to complete the concept map below:

saturated	single bond	aromatic
double bond	unsaturated	triple bond
hydrocarbons	alkane	

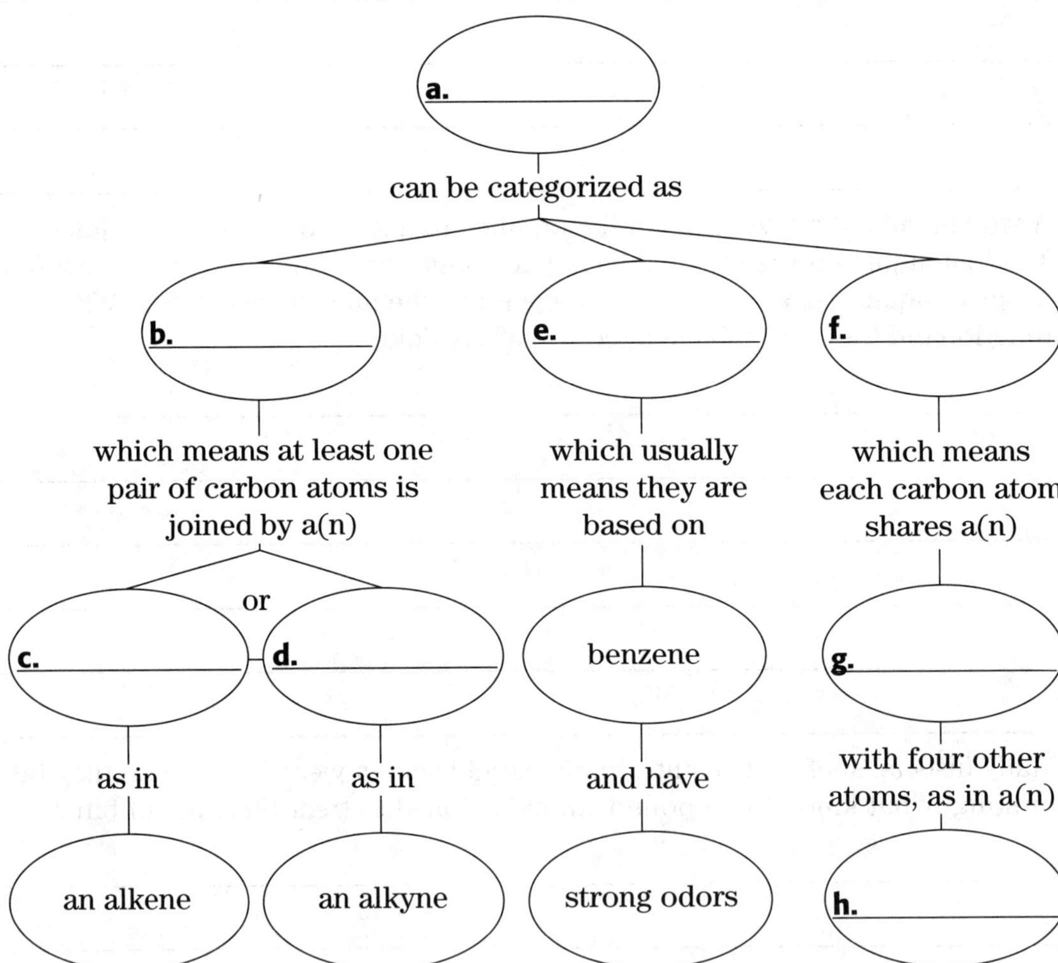

Chapter Test C

Chemical Compounds

MULTIPLE CHOICE

Circle the letter of the best answer for each question.

1. What compounds are brittle and have high melting points?

    a. covalent

    b. organic

    c. ionic

    d. nucleic

2. What force of attraction holds atoms or ions together?

    a. chemical bond

    b. chemical reaction

    c. nucleic acid

    d. neutralization

3. Why should you NEVER taste or touch an unknown acid?

    a. It could be corrosive.

    b. It could be slippery.

    c. It could smell bad.

    d. It could bite you.

4. What do foods that taste sour usually contain?

    a. acid

    b. base

    c. indicator

    d. water

| Chapter Test C *continued*

<u>Circle the letter</u> of the best answer for each question.

5. What compound used in cleaners feels slippery?

   a. acid

   b. sugar

   c. salt

   d. base

6. In what type of solution do all the molecules of an acid break apart in water?

   a. weak acid

   b. strong acid

   c. medium acid

   d. neutral

7. What is left when a base and an acid neutralize?

   a. hydrochloric acid

   b. pH

   c. hydronium ions

   d. water and a salt

8. What kind of melting point do ionic compounds have?

   a. low

   b. neutral

   c. strong

   d. high

9. What type of acid is used to make plastics?

   a. nitric

   b. hydrochloric

   c. sulfuric

   d. carbonic

Chapter Test C *continued*

MATCHING

Read the description. Then, <u>draw a line</u> from the dot next to each description to the matching word.

10. made of sugar molecules ●   **a.** proteins

11. do not dissolve in water ●   **b.** lipids

12. made of amino acids ●   **c.** carbohydrates

13. store genetic information ●   **d.** nucleic acids

---

14. formed by a metal and a
nonmetal ●
            a. hydrocarbons

15. can be saturated or unsaturated ●   **b.** ionic compounds

16 change color depending on
conditions such as pH ●   **c.** covalent compounds

            d. indicators

17. formed by atoms that share an
electron ●

| Chapter Test C *continued*

FILL-IN-THE-BLANK

Read the words in the box. Read the sentences. <u>Fill in each blank</u> with the word or phrase that best completes the sentence.

pH	neutralization reaction	salt

18. A value used to express acidity or alkalinity is

called _______________________.

19. When an acid neutralizes a base, a(n)

_______________________ and water are made.

20. The reaction between acids and bases is called

a(n) _______________________.

biochemicals	organic compounds

21. Over 90% of all compounds are _______________________.

22. Organic compounds made by living things are

called _______________________.

Name _________________________________ Class _______________ Date _____________

Performance-Based Assessment

OBJECTIVE

In this activity you will demonstrate safe lab practices while handling reactive chemical compounds. You will also demonstrate deductive reasoning to identify chemical compounds.

KNOW THE SCORE!

As you work through this activity, keep in mind that you will be earning a grade for the following:

- how well you work with the materials and equipment (40%)
- how well you observe and explain your observations of the different compounds (30%)
- how well you analyze the characteristics of each compound (30%)

Using Scientific Methods

MATERIALS

- 250 mL beakers (4)
- litmus paper (red and blue)
- protective gloves
- salt
- food coloring

SAFETY INFORMATION 

- do not taste, touch or smell the chemicals
- one of the liquids is an acid and another is a base
- notify teacher immediately if a beaker breaks or a student cuts himself or herself
- if any of the liquids spill, immediately flush the area with water
- do not dispose of any liquid until you receive instructions from your teacher

▌Performance-Based Assessment *continued*

ASK A QUESTION

How can you use indicators to identify the pH of an unknown substance?

PROCEDURE

1. Look at the four beakers. Each of these beakers contains a different substance: a base, water, a hydrocarbon, or an acid. Describe the appearance of the liquids in each of the beakers.

____

____

FORM A HYPOTHESIS

2. Try to predict the contents of each beaker by looking at them.

____

____

TEST THE HYPOTHESIS

3. Dip a piece of blue litmus paper into each liquid. What happens?

____

____

4. Dip a piece of red litmus paper into each liquid. Describe what happens.

____

____

5. Write down what you now know about two of the liquids.

____

____

6. Knowing that salt dissolves in water, how can you use salt to identify the last two unknown liquids?

____

____

7. Add salt to the unknown liquids. Stir gently. Describe what happens.

____

____

| Performance-Based Assessment *continued*

8. Knowing that hydrocarbons will not dissolve in water, how could you use food coloring to see if the last unknown liquid is a hydrocarbon?

____

____

9. Add food coloring to the last unknown liquid. Carefully pour it into the liquid that salt dissolved in. Describe what happens.

____

____

10. Write down what you now know about these last two liquids.

____

____

ANALYZE THE RESULTS

11. Identify all of the liquids.

____

____

____

12. How does that compare to your hypothesis? How many of the liquids did you make a correct hypothesis about?

____

____

13. What specific properties of each liquid helped you to identify it?

____

____

Standardized Test Preparation

READING

Read each of the passages. Then, answer the questions that follow each passage.

Passage 1 Spider webs often resemble a bicycle wheel. The "spokes" of the web are made of a silk thread called *dragline silk*. The sticky, stretchy part of the web is called *capture silk* because the spiders use this silk to <u>capture</u> their prey. Spider silk is made of proteins, and proteins are made of amino acids. There are 20 naturally occurring amino acids, but spider silk has only 7 of them. Scientists used a technique called *nuclear magnetic resonance* (NMR) to see the structure of dragline silk. The silk fiber is made of two tough strands of alanine-rich protein embedded in a glycine-rich substance. This protein resembles tangled spaghetti. Scientists believe that this tangled part makes the silk springy and that a repeating sequence of 5 amino acids makes the protein stretchy.

_______ **1.** According to the passage, how many types of amino acids does spider silk contain?

    A 20 amino acids

    B 5 amino acids

    C 7 amino acids

    D all naturally occurring amino acids

_______ **2.** Based on the passage, which of the following statements is a fact?

    F Capture silk makes up the "spokes" of the web.

    G The silk fiber is made of two strands of glycine-rich protein.

    H Proteins are made of amino acids.

    I Spider webs are strong because of a repeating sequence of 5 amino acids.

_______ **3.** In this passage, what does *capture* mean?

    A to kill

    B to eat

    C to free

    D to trap

Standardized Test Preparation *continued*

Passage 2 The earliest evidence of soap-making dates back to 2,800 BCE. A soaplike material was found in clay cylinders in ancient Babylon. According to Roman legend, soap was named after Mount Sapo, where animals were sacrificed. A soaplike substance was made when rain washed the melted animal fat and wood ashes into the clay soil along the Tiber River. In 1791, a major step toward large scale <u>commercial</u> soapmaking began when Nicholas Leblanc, a French chemist, patented a process for making soda ash from salt. About 20 years later, the science of modern soapmaking was born. At that time, Michel Chevreul, another French chemist, discovered how fats, glycerin, and fatty acids interact. This interaction is the basis of saponification, or soap chemistry, today.

_______ **1.** In this passage, what does *commercial* mean?
    A for advertising purposes
    B for public sale
    C from French manufacturers
    D for a limited time period

_______ **2.** Based on the passage, which of the following statements is a fact?
    F Saponification is a process used to make soap.
    G The word *soap* probably originated from the French.
    H Modern soapmaking began around 1791.
    I Soapmaking began 2,000 years ago.

_______ **3.** Which of the following statements is the best summary for the passage?
    A The process of soapmaking has a history of at least 4,000 years.
    B Most of the scientists responsible for soapmaking were from France.
    C Commercial soapmaking began in 1791.
    D Soap chemistry is called *saponification.*

Standardized Test Preparation *continued*

INTERPRETING GRAPHICS

The diagram below shows a model of a water molecule (H_2O). Use the diagram to answer the questions that follow.

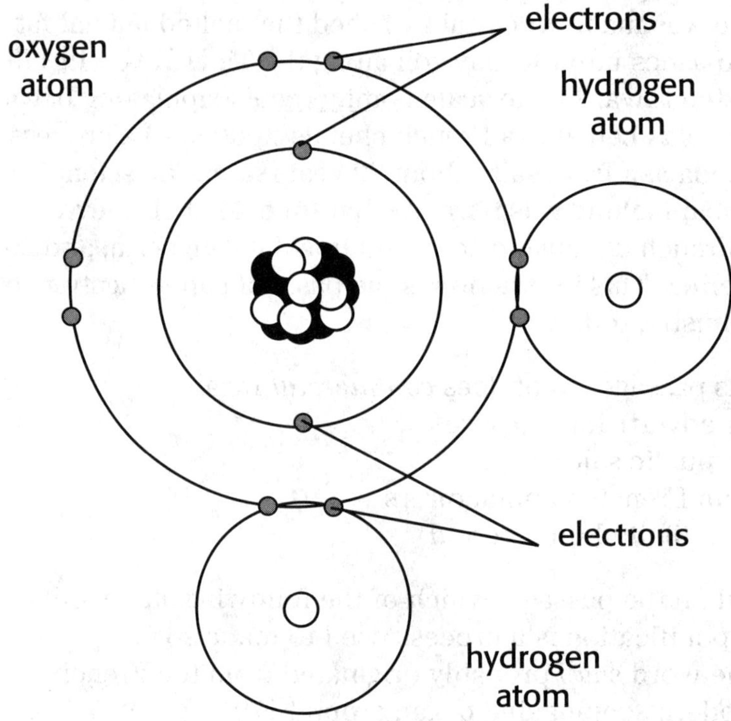

_______ **1.** Which statement best describes the oxygen atom?
  A The oxygen atom has four valence electrons.
  B The oxygen atom is sharing two electrons with two other atoms.
  C The oxygen atom lost two electrons.
  D The oxygen atom has two valence electrons.

_______ **2.** Which of the following features cannot be determined by looking at the model?
  F the number of atoms in the molecule
  G the number of electrons in each atom
  H the type of bonds joining the atoms
  I the physical state of the substance

_______ **3.** Which statement best describes each of the smaller atoms in the molecule?
  A Each atom has eight total electrons.
  B Each atom has two protons.
  C Each atom has two valence electrons.
  D Each atom has lost two electrons.

Name _________________________________ Class _______________ Date _____________

MATH

Read each question below, and choose the best answer.

_______ **1.** Marty is making 8 gal of lemonade. How much sugar does he need if
1 1/2 cups of sugar are needed for every 2 gal of lemonade?
A 4 cups
B 6 cups
C 3 cups
D 8 cups

_______ **2.** The Jimenez family went to the science museum. They bought four
tickets at $12.95 each, four snacks at $3 each, and two souvenirs at
$7.95 each. What is the best estimate of the total cost of tickets,
snacks, and souvenirs?
F $24
G $50
H $63
I $80

_______ **3.** Each whole number on the pH scale represents a tenfold change in the
concentration of hydronium ions. An acid that has a pH of 2 has how
many times more hydronium ions than an acid that has a pH of 5?
A 30 times more hydronium ions
B 100 times more hydronium ions
C 1,000 times more hydronium ions
D 10,000 times more hydronium ions

Skills Practice Lab

Cabbage Patch Indicators

Indicators are weak acids or bases that change color due to the pH of the substance to which they are added. Red cabbage contains a natural indicator. It turns specific colors at specific pHs. In this lab you will extract the indicator from red cabbage. Then, you will use it to determine the pH of several liquids.

OBJECTIVES

Make a natural acid-base indicator solution.

Determine the pH of various common substances.

MATERIALS

- beaker, 250 mL
- beaker tongs
- eyedropper
- hot plate
- litmus paper
- pot holder
- red cabbage leaf
- sample liquids provided by teacher
- tape, masking
- test tubes
- test-tube rack
- water, distilled

SAFETY INFORMATION 

PROCEDURE

1. Use the table below to record your observations. Be sure to include one line for each sample liquid.

Data Collection Table			
Liquid	**Color with indicator**	**pH**	**Effect on litmus paper**
Control			

Cabbage Patch Indicators *continued*

2. Put on protective gloves. Place 100 mL of distilled water in the beaker. Tear the cabbage leaf into small pieces. Place the pieces in the beaker.

3. Use the hot plate to heat the cabbage and water to boiling. Continue boiling until the water is deep blue. **Caution:** Use extreme care when working near a hot plate.

4. Use tongs to remove the beaker from the hot plate. Turn the hot plate off. Allow the solution to cool on a pot holder for 5 to 10 minutes.

5. While the solution is cooling, use masking tape and a pen to label the test tubes for each sample liquid. Label one test tube as the control. Place the tubes in the rack.

6. Use the eyedropper to place a small amount (about 5 mL) of the indicator (cabbage juice) in the test tube labeled as the control.

7. Pour a small amount (about 5 mL) of each sample liquid into the appropriate test tube.

8. Using the eyedropper, place several drops of the indicator into each test tube. Swirl gently. Record the color of each liquid in the table.

9. Use the chart in your book to the find the pH of each sample. Record the pH values in the table.

10. Litmus paper has an indicator that turns red in an acid and blue in a base. Test each liquid with a strip of litmus paper. Record the results.

ANALYZE THE RESULTS

1. **Analyzing Data** What purpose does the control serve? What is the pH of the control?

____

____

____

2. **Examining Data** What colors in your samples indicate the presence of an acid? What colors indicate the presence of a base?

____

____

3. **Analyzing Results** Why is red cabbage juice considered a good indicator?

____

____

____

Cabbage Patch Indicators *continued*

DRAW CONCLUSIONS

4. Interpreting Information Which do you think would be more useful to help
identify an unknown liquid—litmus paper or red cabbage juice? Why?

____

____

____

____

APPLYING YOUR DATA

Unlike distilled water, rainwater has some carbon dioxide dissolved in it. Is
rainwater acidic, basic, or neutral? To find out, place a small amount of the
cabbage juice indicator (which is water-based) in a clean test tube. Use a straw
to gently blow bubbles in the indicator. Continue blowing bubbles until you see
a color change. What can you conclude about the pH of your "rainwater?" What
is the purpose of blowing bubbles in the cabbage juice?

____

____

____

____

____

Name _______________________________ Class _________________ Date ___________

Quick Lab

Blue to Red—Acid!

MATERIALS

- litmus paper, red and blue
- sample solutions, provided by teacher

SAFETY INFORMATION 

PROCEDURES

1. Pour about 5 mL of **test solution** into a **spot plate.** Test the solution using **red litmus paper** and **blue litmus paper** by dipping a **stirring rod** into it and then touching the rod to a piece of litmus paper.

2. Record any color changes. Clean the stirring rod.

____

____

____

____

3. Repeat the above steps with each solution. Use new pieces of litmus paper as needed.

4. Identify each solution as acidic or basic.

____

____

____

____

Quick Lab

pHast Relief

MATERIALS

- antacid tablet
- litmus paper, red and blue
- plastic cup, small
- vinegar

SAFETY INFORMATION 

PROCEDURE

1. Pour **vinegar** into a **small plastic cup** until the cup is half full. Test the vinegar with **red** and **blue litmus paper.** record your results

   ____

   ____

2. Crush one **antacid tablet,** and mix it with the vinegar. Test the mixture with litmus paper. Record your results.

   ____

   ____

3. Compare the acidity of the solution before the antacid was added with the acidity of the solution after it was added.

   ____

   ____

   ____

Quick Lab

Food Facts

MATERIALS

- food packages, empty (4)

PROCEDURE

1. Select four empty **food packages.**

2. Without reading the Nutrition Facts labels, rank the items from most carbohydrate content to least carbohydrate content.

____

____

____

3. Rank the items from most fat content to least fat content.

____

____

____

4. Read the Nutrition Facts labels, and compare your rankings with the real rankings.

____

____

____

5. Why do you think your rankings were right or were wrong? Explain your answer.

____

____

____

____

____

Skills Practice Lab

Making Salt

A neutralization reaction between an acid and a base produces water and a salt. In this lab, you will react an acid with a base and then let the water evaporate. You will then examine what is left for properties that tell you that it is indeed a salt.

MATERIALS

- beaker, 100 mL
- eyedroppers (2)
- evaporating dish
- gloves, protective
- graduated cylinder, 100 mL
- hydrochloric acid
- magnifying lens
- phenolphthalein solution in a dropper bottle
- stirring rod, glass
- sodium hydroxide
- water, distilled

SAFETY INFORMATION 

Using Scientific Methods

ASK A QUESTION

1. Write a question about reactions between acids and bases.

____

FORM A HYPOTHESIS

2. Write a hypothesis that may answer the question you asked in the step above.

____

____

TEST THE HYPOTHESIS

3. Put on protective gloves. Carefully measure 25 mL of hydrochloric acid in a graduated cylinder, and then pour it into the beaker. Carefully rinse the graduated cylinder with distilled water to clean out any leftover acid. **Caution:** Hydrochloric acid is corrosive. If any should spill on you, immediately flush the area with water, and notify your teacher.

4. Add 3 drops of phenolphthalein indicator to the acid in the beaker. You will not see anything happen yet because this indicator won't show its color unless too much base is present.

5. Measure 20 mL of sodium hydroxide (base) in the graduated cylinder, and add it slowly to the beaker with the acid. Use the stirring rod to mix the substances completely. **Caution:** Sodium hydroxide is also corrosive. If any should spill on you, immediately flush the area with water, and notify your teacher.

6. Use an eyedropper to add more base, a few drops at a time, to the acid-base mixture in the beaker. Be sure to stir the mixture after each few drops. Continue adding drops of base until the mixture remains colored after stirring.

7. Use another eyedropper to add acid to the beaker, 1 drop at a time, until the color just disappears after stirring.

8. Pour the mixture carefully into an evaporating dish, and place the dish where your teacher tells you to allow the water to evaporate overnight.

9. The next day, examine your evaporating dish, and with a magnifying lens, study the crystals that were left. Identify the color, shape, and other properties of the crystals.

ANALYZE THE RESULTS

1. The following equation is for the reaction that occurred in this experiment:

$$HCl + NaOH \rightarrow H_2O + NaCl$$

NaCl is ordinary table salt and forms very regular cubic crystals that are white. Did you find white cubic crystals?

____

____

2. The phenolphthalein indicator changes color in the presence of a base. Why did you add more acid in step 7 until the color disappeared?

____

____

APPLYING YOUR DATA

Another neutralization reaction occurs between hydrochloric acid and potassium hydroxide, KOH. The equation for this reaction is as follows:

$$HCl + KOH \rightarrow H_2O + KCl$$

What are the products of this neutralization reaction? How do they compare with those you discovered in this experiment?

____

____

____

Activity

Vocabulary Activity

Compounding the Problem

Use the clues below and on the next page to identify vocabulary items from the chapter. Then, find and circle each item in the word search puzzle on the next page. Remember to look backwards and diagonally also!

1. These organic compounds are made of carbon and hydrogen.

____

2. Atoms share electrons in this type of compound.

____

3. These organic compounds are sometimes called the "blueprints of life."

____

4. This is the measure of the concentration of hydronium ions in a solution.

____

5. Plants store these as oils.

____

6. The positive ion of a base and the negative ion of an acid combine to form this type of ionic compound.

____

7. This substance increases the number of H_3O^+ when dissolved in water.

____

8. These organic compounds are made by living things.

____

9. This substance feels slippery and tastes bitter.

____

10. These biochemicals are composed of one or more simple sugar molecules bonded together.

____

11. These compounds contain oppositely charged ions arranged in a crystal lattice.

____

12. These most common of all compounds are composed of molecules whose atoms are arranged in a straight chain, a branched chain, or a ring.

____

13. These biochemicals have many functions in the body, such as regulating chemical activities.

____

14. This special paper is used to test for acids and bases.

____

15. These are building blocks of a protein.

____

Vocabulary Activity *continued*

16. This protein regulates the amount of glucose in your blood.

____

17. This type of carbohydrate has hundreds of thousands of sugar molecules.

____

18. This compound can reversibly change color depending on conditions such as pH.

____

19. A carbon atom can form no more than this number of bonds.

____

20. This type of nucleic acid is the genetic material of the cell.

____

21. This type of hydrocarbon contains carbon atoms connected only by a single bond.

____

22. This protein carries oxygen to all parts of your body.

____

23. The combining of atoms to form molecules results in this

____

Y	X	B	H	T	A	R	O	T	A	C	I	D	N	I	A
J	C	E	I	P	N	X	A	B	R	M	W	S	O	N	L
A	H	I	L	O	T	E	I	O	B	I	A	E	D	I	T
S	W	L	N	P	C	L	P	N	I	L	S	C	P	I	L
N	S	R	A	A	M	H	A	D	X	A	A	I	N	Y	N
O	D	S	C	G	G	O	E	S	B	R	D	I	D	C	I
B	I	N	K	A	A	R	C	M	B	S	L	M	V	H	B
R	C	I	Z	V	U	U	O	O	I	U	W	N	U	P	O
A	A	E	J	O	E	Y	H	C	S	C	Q	P	H	G	L
C	O	T	F	A	E	Y	O	N	A	L	A	E	T	X	G
O	N	O	V	W	D	V	I	H	H	C	I	L	I	G	O
R	I	R	L	R	A	I	X	Y	F	M	I	T	S	Q	M
D	M	P	A	L	O	J	K	V	K	K	T	D	M	H	E
Y	A	T	E	N	G	L	V	P	B	E	D	U	Q	U	H
H	E	N	I	N	B	D	E	T	A	R	U	T	A	S	S
S	T	C	N	U	C	L	E	I	C	A	C	I	D	S	R

SciLinks Activity

Acids and Bases

Go to www.scilinks.org. To find links related to acids and bases type in the keyword HSM0013. Then browse the links to find information on acids and bases. Use links to answer the following items.

1. Draw a pH scale that starts at 1 and goes to 12. Then, browse the links to find the pH of at least 10 different substances and write their name and pH on the scale.

2. Describe some of the chemical effects of acids and bases.

____

____

____

____

3. List some of the substances you identified in question 1 and describe how we make use of their chemical properties.

____

____

____

____

____

Performance-Based Assessment

Teacher Notes and Answer Key

PURPOSE

Students will use lab materials and deductive reasoning to identify four different chemical compounds.

TIME REQUIRED

One 45-minute class period

Students will need 30 minutes to perform the procedure and 15 minutes to answer analysis questions.

RATINGS

Teacher Prep–3
Student Set-Up–2
Concept Level–2
Clean Up–3

ADVANCE PREPARATION

It may be necessary to order some chemicals in advance. Equip each activity station with the necessary materials. Put the sodium hydroxide (0.5 M), baby oil, hydrochloric acid (0.5 M), and water into 250 mL beakers labeled "Liquid A," "Liquid B," "Liquid C," and "Liquid D," respectively. When making the solutions, always add the acid or base to the water.

SAFETY INFORMATION

Remind students not to taste, touch, or smell the chemicals. Warn students that one of the liquids is an acid and another is a base. Students should immediately notify the teacher if a beaker breaks or if a student cuts himself or herself. Ensure that the beakers do not have chips or cracks. If any of the liquids spill, immediately flush the area with water. To dispose of the hydrochloric acid and sodium hydroxide, combine them until the pH is between 6 and 8. Then pour the mixture down the drain.

TEACHING STRATEGIES

Emphasis must be placed on the safety information for this activity. This activity works best in groups of four students. The acid and base should be in dilute concentrations as indicated above. Review the characteristics of an acid, base, hydrocarbon, and water. Remind students how to distinguish between an acid and a base using blue and red litmus paper.

Performance-Based Assessment *continued*

Evaluation Strategies

Use the following rubric to help evaluate student performance.

Rubric for Assessment

Possible points	Appropriate use of materials and equipment (40 points possible)
40–30	Task is complete; safe and careful handling of materials and equipment; attention to detain; superior lab skills
29–15	Task is generally complete; successful use of materials and equipment; sound knowledge of lab techniques; somewhat unfocused performance; mild neglect of safety measures
14–1	Task is incomplete; yields inadequate results; sloppy lab technique; apparent lack of skill
	Quality and clarity of observations (30 points possible)
30–20	Superior observations stated clearly and accurately; high level of detail
19–15	Accurate observations; moderate level of detail; correct use of units of measurement
14–10	Complete observations, but expressed in unclear manner; may include minor inaccuracies
9–1	Erroneous, incomplete, or unclear observations; lack of accuracy or details
	Analysis of compounds (30 points possible)
30–20	Clear, detailed explanation shows superior knowledge of the properties of compounds; use of examples to support explanations
19–10	Adequate understanding of properties of compounds with minor difficulty in expression
9–1	Poor understanding of the properties of compounds; explanation unclear or not relevant to compound properties; substantial factual errors

Name _______________________________ Class _______________ Date _______________

Performance-Based Assessment

OBJECTIVE

In this activity you will demonstrate safe lab practices while handling reactive chemical compounds. You will also demonstrate deductive reasoning to identify chemical compounds.

KNOW THE SCORE!

As you work through this activity, keep in mind that you will be earning a grade for the following:

- how well you work with the materials and equipment (40%)
- how well you observe and explain your observations of the different compounds (30%)
- how well you analyze the characteristics of each compound (30%)

Using Scientific Methods

MATERIALS

- 250 mL beakers (4)
- litmus paper (red and blue)
- protective gloves
- salt
- food coloring

SAFETY INFORMATION 

- do not taste, touch or smell the chemicals
- one of the liquids is an acid and another is a base
- notify teacher immediately if a beaker breaks or a student cuts himself or herself
- if any of the liquids spill, immediately flush the area with water
- do not dispose of any liquid until you receive instructions from your teacher

Name _______________________________ Class _______________ Date ____________

Performance-Based Assessment *continued*

ASK A QUESTION

How can you use indicators to identify the pH of an unknown substance?

PROCEDURE

1. Look at the four beakers. Each of these beakers contains a different substance: a base, water, a hydrocarbon, or an acid. Describe the appearance of the liquids in each of the beakers.

   Liquid A: colorless, thin like water; Liquid B: colorless, viscous with bubbles;

   Liquid C: colorless, thin like water; Liquid D; colorless, thin like water.

FORM A HYPOTHESIS

2. Try to predict the contents of each beaker by looking at them.

   Predictions will vary.

TEST THE HYPOTHESIS

3. Dip a piece of blue litmus paper into each liquid. What happens?

   Liquid C turns the litmus paper pink. The litmus paper remains blue in the

   other liquids.

4. Dip a piece of red litmus paper into each liquid. Describe what happens.

   Liquid A turns the litmus paper blue. The litmus paper remains red in the

   other liquids.

5. Write down what you now know about two of the liquids.

   Liquid C is the acid; Liquid A is the base.

6. Knowing that salt dissolves in water, how can you use salt to identify the last two unknown liquids?

   I can add salt to both and see which one dissolves the salt.

7. Add salt to the unknown liquids. Stir gently. Describe what happens.

   The salt dissolves in Liquid D.

Name _________________________ Class _______________ Date _________

Performance-Based Assessment *continued*

8. Knowing that hydrocarbons will not dissolve in water, how could you use food coloring to see if the last unknown liquid is a hydrocarbon?

Add food coloring to one of the liquids, and combine them. The hydrocarbon

will float on the water.

9. Add food coloring to the last unknown liquid. Carefully pour it into the liquid that salt dissolved in. Describe what happens.

The liquid with the food coloring rises to the top of the beaker.

ANALYZE THE RESULTS

11. Identify all of the liquids.

Liquid A is the base, Liquid B is the hydrocarbon, Liquid C is the acid, and

Liquid D is the water.

12. How does that compare to your hypothesis? How many of the liquids did you make a correct hypothesis about?

Answers will vary. Answers will include the hypothesis and a comparison.

13. What specific properties of each liquid helped you to identify it?

solubility, color

DATASHEET FOR CHAPTER LAB

Cabbage Patch Indicators

Teacher Notes and Answer Key

TIME REQUIRED

One 45-minute class period

LAB RATINGS

Easy ← 1 2 3 4 → Hard

Teacher Prep–2
Student Set-Up–2
Concept Level–2
Clean Up–2

MATERIALS

Materials listed are for groups of 2–3 students. Choose a wide variety of sample liquids, including bleach, ammonia, clear soda pop, lemon juice, milk, and baking soda (dissolved in water). Either red or blue litmus paper (or both) will work.

SAFETY CAUTION

Remind students to review all safety cautions and icons before beginning this lab activity. Caution students to use care when using the hot plate. Have students use tongs when handling the beaker with the hot water. Tell students that even diluted acids and bases can irritate the skin. Students should wash the affected area immediately if any sample liquid touches their skin.

DISPOSAL INFORMATION

Use the appropriate disposal technique for each sample liquid.

Name _________________________________ Class _______________ Date ___________

DATASHEET FOR CHAPTER LAB

Cabbage Patch Indicators

Indicators are weak acids or bases that change color due to the pH of the substance to which they are added. Red cabbage contains a natural indicator. It turns specific colors at specific pHs. In this lab you will extract the indicator from red cabbage. Then, you will use it to determine the pH of several liquids.

OBJECTIVES

Make a natural acid-base indicator solution.

Determine the pH of various common substances.

MATERIALS

- beaker, 250 mL
- beaker tongs
- eyedropper
- hot plate
- litmus paper
- pot holder
- red cabbage leaf
- sample liquids provided by teacher
- tape, masking
- test tubes
- test-tube rack
- water, distilled

SAFETY INFORMATION    

PROCEDURE

1. Use the table below to record your observations. Be sure to include one line for each sample liquid.

Data Collection Table			
Liquid	**Color with indicator**	**pH**	**Effect on litmus paper**
Control			

Name _______________________________ Class _______________ Date _____________

Cabbage Patch Indicators *continued*

2. Put on protective gloves. Place 100 mL of distilled water in the beaker. Tear the cabbage leaf into small pieces. Place the pieces in the beaker.

3. Use the hot plate to heat the cabbage and water to boiling. Continue boiling until the water is deep blue. **Caution:** Use extreme care when working near a hot plate.

4. Use tongs to remove the beaker from the hot plate. Turn the hot plate off. Allow the solution to cool on a pot holder for 5 to 10 minutes.

5. While the solution is cooling, use masking tape and a pen to label the test tubes for each sample liquid. Label one test tube as the control. Place the tubes in the rack.

6. Use the eyedropper to place a small amount (about 5 mL) of the indicator (cabbage juice) in the test tube labeled as the control.

7. Pour a small amount (about 5 mL) of each sample liquid into the appropriate test tube.

8. Using the eyedropper, place several drops of the indicator into each test tube. Swirl gently. Record the color of each liquid in the table.

9. Use the chart in your book to the find the pH of each sample. Record the pH values in the table.

10. Litmus paper has an indicator that turns red in an acid and blue in a base. Test each liquid with a strip of litmus paper. Record the results.

ANALYZE THE RESULTS

1. Analyzing Data What purpose does the control serve? What is the pH of the control?

The control serves as a color comparison for test tubes containing the

sample liquids. The control is reddish blue, which indicates that it is neutral,

so the pH is about 7.

2. Examining Data What colors in your samples indicate the presence of an acid? What colors indicate the presence of a base?

Reddish colors indicate acids; bluish colors indicate bases.

3. Analyzing Results Why is red cabbage juice considered a good indicator?

Red cabbage juice is a good indicator because its color can indicate many pH

values. It can be used to identify the relative strengths of acids and bases

if their concentrations are the same.

Name _______________________________ Class _______________ Date _____________

Cabbage Patch Indicators *continued*

DRAW CONCLUSIONS

4. Interpreting Information Which do you think would be more useful to help identify an unknown liquid—litmus paper or red cabbage juice? Why?

Red cabbage juice—it would give you an approximate idea of the pH of the

unknown liquid. The pH could then be used to help identify the substance.

Litmus paper can indicate only whether the unknown liquid is acidic or

basic.

APPLYING YOUR DATA

Unlike distilled water, rainwater has some carbon dioxide dissolved in it. Is rainwater acidic, basic, or neutral? To find out, place a small amount of the cabbage juice indicator (which is water-based) in a clean test tube. Use a straw to gently blow bubbles in the indicator. Continue blowing bubbles until you see a color change. What can you conclude about the pH of your "rainwater?" What is the purpose of blowing bubbles in the cabbage juice?

Students should find that rainwater is slightly acidic. Blowing bubbles

dissolves carbon dioxide in the cabbage juice.

Name ___________________________   Class _______________   Date ___________

  DATASHEET FOR QUICK LAB

Blue to Red–Acid!

MATERIALS

- litmus paper, red and blue
- sample solutions, provided by teacher

SAFETY INFORMATION 

PROCEDURES

1. Pour about 5 mL of **test solution** into a **spot plate.** Test the solution using **red litmus paper** and **blue litmus paper** by dipping a **stirring rod** into it and then touching the rod to a piece of litmus paper.

2. Record any color changes. Clean the stirring rod.

____

____

____

____

3. Repeat the above steps with each solution. Use new pieces of litmus paper as needed.

4. Identify each solution as acidic or basic.

Answers may vary. Acids turn blue litmus red. Bases turn red litmus blue.

____

____

____

Name _______________________________ Class _______________ Date _____________

DATASHEET FOR QUICK LAB

pHast Relief

MATERIALS

- antacid tablet
- litmus paper, red and blue
- plastic cup, small
- vinegar

SAFETY INFORMATION 

PROCEDURE

1. Pour **vinegar** into a **small plastic cup** until the cup is half full. Test the vinegar with **red** and **blue litmus paper.** record your results

   ____

   ____

2. Crush one **antacid tablet,** and mix it with the vinegar. Test the mixture with litmus paper. Record your results.

   ____

   ____

3. Compare the acidity of the solution before the antacid was added with the acidity of the solution after it was added.

   The vinegar was more acidic before the reaction than the mixture was after

   the reaction.

   ____

SAFETY CAUTION Remind students to review all safety cautions and icons before beginning this lab activity.

Name _______________________________ Class _______________ Date ___________

DATASHEET FOR QUICK LAB

Food Facts

MATERIALS

- food packages, empty (4)

PROCEDURE

1. Select four empty **food packages.**

2. Without reading the Nutrition Facts labels, rank the items from most carbohydrate content to least carbohydrate content.

   ____

   ____

   ____

3. Rank the items from most fat content to least fat content.

   ____

   ____

   ____

4. Read the Nutrition Facts labels, and compare your rankings with the real rankings.

   ____

   ____

   ____

5. Why do you think your rankings were right or were wrong? Explain your answer.

   Accept all reasonable answers. ___________________________________

   ____

   ____

   ____

   ____

   ____

Making Salt

DATASHEET FOR LABBOOK

Teacher Notes and Answer Key

TIME REQUIRED

One 45-minute class period, plus 10 minutes the following day

Rodney A. Sandefur
Naturita Middle School
Naturita, Colorado

LAB RATINGS

Easy ◄——1——2——3——4——► Hard

Teacher Prep–2
Student Set-Up–2
Concept Level–2
Clean Up–2

PROCEDURE NOTES

You may wish to do this lab as a demonstration or class activity if time or materials are limited.

SAFETY CAUTION

Review all proper safety precautions with your students. Students should wear safety goggles, protective gloves, and an apron. In case of an acid or a base spill, first dilute the spill with water. Then, while wearing disposable plastic gloves, mop up the spill with wet cloths designated for spill cleanup. A wet cloth mop can be rinsed out a few times and used until it falls apart. Work with another person nearby who can call for help in case of an emergency, and work near (no more than a few seconds away from) a safety shower and eyewash station known to be in operating condition.

Hydrochloric Acid Use only concentrations of hydrochloric acid below 1.0 M. Students should not handle concentrated solutions. Avoid contact with skin and eyes, and avoid breathing vapors. When making a solution, it is important always to add the acid to the water so that if something splashes out, it will most likely be water.

Sodium Hydroxide Use only concentrations of sodium hydroxide below 1.0 M. Students should not handle concentrated solutions. Avoid contact with skin and eyes. You should wear goggles, a face shield, impermeable gloves, and a lab apron if you must prepare a solution of NaOH.

Phenolphthalein Students should use only pre-mixed solutions (2 g in 100 mL 95% ethanol; add 100 mL water). Phenolphthalein solutions are flammable, and the vapors can explode when mixed with air. Ensure that there are no flames or sources of ignition, such as sparks, when you are using the phenolphthalein solution. Restrict the amount of phenolphthalein in the room to 100 mL. Caution students not to taste the salt they create—it will have phenolphthalein in it.

Making Salt *continued*

DISPOSAL INFORMATION

Hydrochloric Acid Titrate with 0.1 M NaOH as required until the pH is between 6 and 8, and then pour down the drain.

Sodium Hydroxide Titrate with 0.1 M HCl as required until the pH is between 5 and 9, and then pour down the drain.

Phenolphthalein Set out a container for any used indicator solutions that are left over at the end of the procedure. Titrate the mixture with 0.1 M HCl or 0.1 M NaOH as required until the pH is between 6 and 8, and then pour down the drain. Unused indicators should be tightly covered and returned to the storage shelf.

Name _______________________________ Class _______________ Date _______________

Skills Practice Lab

DATASHEET FOR LABBOOK

Making Salt

A neutralization reaction between an acid and a base produces water and a salt. In this lab, you will react an acid with a base and then let the water evaporate. You will then examine what is left for properties that tell you that it is indeed a salt.

MATERIALS

- beaker, 100 mL
- eyedroppers (2)
- evaporating dish
- gloves, protective
- graduated cylinder, 100 mL
- hydrochloric acid

- magnifying lens
- phenolphthalein solution in a dropper bottle
- stirring rod, glass
- sodium hydroxide
- water, distilled

SAFETY INFORMATION

Using Scientific Methods

ASK A QUESTION

1. Write a question about reactions between acids and bases.

____

FORM A HYPOTHESIS

2. Write a hypothesis that may answer the question you asked in the step above.

____

____

TEST THE HYPOTHESIS

3. Put on protective gloves. Carefully measure 25 mL of hydrochloric acid in a graduated cylinder, and then pour it into the beaker. Carefully rinse the graduated cylinder with distilled water to clean out any leftover acid. **Caution:** Hydrochloric acid is corrosive. If any should spill on you, immediately flush the area with water, and notify your teacher.

4. Add 3 drops of phenolphthalein indicator to the acid in the beaker. You will not see anything happen yet because this indicator won't show its color unless too much base is present.

5. Measure 20 mL of sodium hydroxide (base) in the graduated cylinder, and add it slowly to the beaker with the acid. Use the stirring rod to mix the substances completely. **Caution:** Sodium hydroxide is also corrosive. If any should spill on you, immediately flush the area with water, and notify your teacher.

     101   Chemical Compounds

Name _______________________________ Class _______________ Date _____________

Making Salt *continued*

6. Use an eyedropper to add more base, a few drops at a time, to the acid-base mixture in the beaker. Be sure to stir the mixture after each few drops. Continue adding drops of base until the mixture remains colored after stirring.

7. Use another eyedropper to add acid to the beaker, 1 drop at a time, until the color just disappears after stirring.

8. Pour the mixture carefully into an evaporating dish, and place the dish where your teacher tells you to allow the water to evaporate overnight.

9. The next day, examine your evaporating dish, and with a magnifying lens, study the crystals that were left. Identify the color, shape, and other properties of the crystals.

ANALYZE THE RESULTS

1. The following equation is for the reaction that occurred in this experiment:

$$HCl + NaOH \rightarrow H_2O + NaCl$$

NaCl is ordinary table salt and forms very regular cubic crystals that are white. Did you find white cubic crystals?

Students should observe white cubic crystals.

2. The phenolphthalein indicator changes color in the presence of a base. Why did you add more acid in step 7 until the color disappeared?

The phenolphthalein changing color in step 6 meant that too much base was

present. Acid was added to bring the solution back to neutral.

APPLYING YOUR DATA

Another neutralization reaction occurs between hydrochloric acid and potassium hydroxide, KOH. The equation for this reaction is as follows:

$$HCl + KOH \rightarrow H_2O + KCl$$

What are the products of this neutralization reaction? How do they compare with those you discovered in this experiment?

The products are water and a salt, KCl (potassium chloride).

Answer Key

Directed Reading A

SECTION: IONIC AND COVALENT COMPOUNDS

1. C
2. A
3. B
4. A
5. C
6. B
7. A
8. B
9. C
10. C
11. C
12. The ions are charged and able to move freely past one another.
13. D
14. A
15. C
16. The substance doesn't dissolve or mix well in water.
17. The attraction of water molecules for each other is greater than their attraction for covalent molecules.
18. The force of attraction between covalent molecules is much weaker than the attraction between ionic compounds, so covalent molecules melt at lower temperatures.
19. Sugar does not have charged particles or form ions when it dissolves in water
20. Many acids form ions in water. These solutions, like ionic substances, conduct an electric current.

SECTION: ACIDS AND BASES

1. B
2. B
3. B
4. C
5. C
6. D
7. A
8. C
9. B
10. D
11. C
12. B
13. A
14. D
15. C
16. E
17. D
18. B
19. C
20. A
21. C
22. B
23. A
24. C

SECTION: SOLUTIONS OF ACIDS AND BASES

1. A
2. D
3. A
4. C
5. B
6. D
7. A
8. B
9. A
10. pH
11. hydronium
12. 7
13. basic
14. acidic
15. Answers will include three of the following: sea water, detergents, household ammonia, tap water
16. Answers will include three of the following: lemon juice, soft drink, milk, human saliva, acid rain, clear rain, human stomach contents
17. 4-6
18. 8-9
19. about 7
20. Answers will vary. Sample answer: Rainwater reacts with compounds in air pollution, creating acids and lowering rainwater's pH. This acid rain collects in lakes, killing fish and other organisms.
21. water and salt
22. Salt is an ionic compound formed from the positive ion of a base and the negative ion of an acid.
23. Answers will vary. Sample answer: sodium chloride, to season food; sodium nitrate, to preserve food; calcium sulfate, to make wall board.

SECTION: ORGANIC COMPOUNDS

1. C
2. D
3. B
4. A
5. C
6. B
7. B
8. A
9. C
10. D
11. benzene
12. alternating single and double bonds
13. a strong odor
14. Answers will include three of the following: halogens, oxygen, sulfur, phosphorous

15. D
16. B
17. C
18. A
19. B
20. C
21. B
22. D
23. Answers will include three of the following: regulate chemical reactions in the body; regulate blood-sugar levels; deliver oxygen throughout the body; transport materials in and out of cells; provide structural support.
24. nucleic acids
25. nucleotides
26. Each living thing has a different order of nucleotides.
27. the blueprints of life
28. Answers will vary. Sample answer: The two kinds of nucleic acids are DNA and RNA. DNA is the genetic material of the cell. RNA is involved in building protein needed by the cell.

Directed Reading B

SECTION: IONIC AND COVALENT COMPOUNDS

1. B
2. D
3. ions
4. ionic compounds
5. metals
6. B
7. D
8. ionic
9. temperatures
10. B
11. C
12. B
13. C
14. A
15. B
16. A
17. A
18. C
19. B
20. C

SECTION: ACIDS AND BASES

1. B
2. D
3. C
4. acids
5. citric
6. corrosive
7. D
8. A
9. B
10. C
11. C
12. B
13. D
14. A
15. B
16. A
17. D
18. B
19. D
20. D
21. B
22. C
23. A

SECTION: SOLUTIONS OF ACIDS AND BASES

1. C
2. D
3. A
4. C
5. neutralization
6. water
7. salt
8. B
9. B
10. A
11. B
12. A
13. B
14. A
15. C
16. D
17. B
18. B
19. C
20. A
21. C
22. B
23. A

SECTION: ORGANIC COMPOUNDS

1. A
2. C
3. C
4. D
5. D
6. C
7. A
8. unsaturated
9. electrons
10. alkenes
11. alkynes
12. B
13. C
14. D
15. C
16. carbohydrates
17. plants
18. simple
19. complex
20. B
21. A
22. proteins
23. amino acids
24. sulfur
25. catalysts
26. hemoglobin
27. nucleic acids
28. nucleotides
29. C
30. B
31. A

Vocabulary and Section Summary

SECTION: IONIC AND COVALENT COMPOUNDS

1. chemical bond: an interaction that holds atoms or ions together
2. ionic compound: a compound made of oppositely charged ions
3. covalent compound: a chemical compound formed by the sharing of electrons

SECTION: ACIDS AND BASES

1. acid: any compound that increases the number of hydronium ions when dissolved in water
2. indicator: a compound that can reversibly change color depending on conditions such as pH
3. base: any compound that increases the number of hydroxide ions when dissolved in water

SECTION: SOLUTIONS OF ACIDS AND BASES

1. neutralization reaction: the reaction of an acid and a base to form a neutral solution of water and salt
2. pH: a value that is used to express the acidity or basicity (alkalinity) of a system
3. salt: an ionic compound that forms when a metal atom replaces the hydrogen of an acid

SECTION: ORGANIC COMPOUNDS

1. organic compound: a covalently bonded compound that contains carbon
2. hydrocarbon: an organic compound composed only of carbon and hydrogen
3. carbohydrate: a class of energy-giving nutrients that includes sugars, starches, and fiber
4. lipid: a type of biochemical that does not dissolve in water, including fats and steroids
5. protein: an organic compound that is made of one or more chains of amino acids and that is a principal component of all cells

6. nucleic acid: an organic compound, either RNA or DNA, whose molecules are made up of one or two chains of nucleotides and carry genetic information

Section Reviews

SECTION: IONIC AND COVALENT COMPOUNDS

1. Answers will vary. Sample answer: Table salt is an ionic compound. Water is a covalent compound. The sodium ion and the chlorine ion in sodium chloride are held together by a chemical bond.
2. C
3. Sample answer: Two properties of covalent compounds are a low melting point and low solubility.
4. $100\% - 39.37\% - 38.10\% = 22.53\%$
5. A solution of ionic crystals in water can conduct an electric current because the ions are charged and are able to move freely past one another. But when ionic crystals are not in solution, their ions cannot move freely and therefore cannot conduct an electric current.
6. The solid is a covalent compound because covalent compounds do not conduct an electric current when dissolved in water.

SECTION: ACIDS AND BASES

1. Answers will vary. Sample answer: An acid is a compound that increases the number of hydronium ions when dissolved in water. A base is a compound that increases the number of hydroxide ions when dissolved in water. An indicator is something that changes color in the presence of an acid or base.
2. A
3. C
4. Red litmus paper turns blue when it touches a base.
5. $472\ mL = 0.472\ L \times 1.06\ qt \times 4\ cups = 2\ cups$

6. Answers will vary. Sample answer: Acids have a sour flavor, change the color of indicators, react with metals, and conduct electric current. Bases have a bitter flavor, feel slippery, change the color of indicators, and conduct electric current.

7. Sample answer: A gardener or a farmer might use litmus paper to test soil samples to see if the soil is acid or base.

8. Answers will vary. Sample answer: I would test the solution with red and blue litmus paper and I would put zinc in the solution. If the solution is an acid, it should turn the blue litmus paper red and should react with the zinc. If the solution is a base, it should turn the red litmus paper blue and should not react with the zinc.

SECTION: SOLUTIONS OF ACIDS AND BASES

1. Answers will vary. Sample answer: A salt and water are produced during a neutralization reaction.

2. D

3. A strong acid is one in which all the molecules of the acid break apart when dissolved in water. A weak acid is one in which only a few molecules break apart when dissolved in water.

4. one hundred times (Students may solve this by noting that there is a two point difference between pH 2 and pH 4, and thinking that each point is considered to be 10. So, $10 \times 10 = 100$.)

5. The hydrogen ion concentration will increase when HCl is added to water. The pH will decrease below pH 7, due to the increased hydrogen ion concentration.

6. No, fish would not be healthy in a lake with a low pH because fish need water that is near pH 7. Fish may die in a lake with a low pH.

7. I would expect the pH of soap to be 9 rather than 4 because soap is made from a base and bases have pHs higher than 7.

SECTION: ORGANIC COMPOUNDS

1. Sample answer: A hydrocarbon and a biochemical are each a type of organic compound.

2. Answers will vary. Sample answer: A carbohydrate is a biochemical composed of simple sugar molecules bonded together. A lipid is a biochemical that does not dissolve in water. A protein is a biochemical that is composed of amino acids. A nucleic acid is a biochemical that is made up of nucleotides.

3. A

4. Sample answer: Functions of proteins include regulating chemical activities, transporting and storing materials, and providing structural support. (Note: students need to list only two functions to answer this question correctly.

5. An aromatic hydrocarbon is a hydrocarbon that is based on benzene.

6. Answers will vary. Sample answer: If there is a mistake in the information needed to make hemoglobin, a cell will not be able to make hemoglobin properly. And if hemoglobin is not made properly it may not be able to transport oxygen to the tissues of the body.

7. Saturated hydrocarbons have only single bonds. Unsaturated hydrocarbons contain at least one double bond or one triple bond.

8. Single bonds are present in the molecule. (Another acceptable answer: Covalent bonds are present in the molecule.)

9. Yes, the shape of the molecule is a straight chain because all the carbon atoms are connected in a straight line.

Chapter Review

1. An ionic compound contains ionic bonds formed by atoms gaining or losing one or more electrons. A covalent compound contains covalent bonds formed by atoms sharing electrons.

2. An acid increases the number of hydronium ions when dissolved in water and a base increases the number of hydroxide ions when dissolved in water.

3. pH is the measure of the hydronium ion concentration in a solution and an indicator is a substance that changes color in the presence of an acid or a base.

4. A hydrocarbon is a compound composed only of hydrogen and carbon and an organic compound is a carbon-based compound that may contain hydrogen, oxygen, sulfur, nitrogen, or phosphorus.

5. A carbohydrate is composed of sugar molecules and a lipid is a biochemical that does not dissolve in water.

6. A protein is composed of amino acids and a nucleic acid is made of nucleotides.

7. D

8. B

9. B

10. C

11. Potassium hydroxide is a base, so I would use an acid to neutralize it.

12. When an acid reacts with a base, the pH of the solution gets closer to pH 7, which indicates a neutral solution.

13. Each carbon atom has four valence electrons and can form four bonds. These bonds can be made to atoms of carbon or to atoms of other elements.

14. Acids produce hydronium ions in water. Bases produce hydroxide ions in water.

15. 473 mL × 5% = 473 mL × 0.05 = 23.65 mL acetic acid;
473 mL − 23.65 mL = 449.35 mL water

16. 75 mL ÷ 300 mL × 100% = 25% juice

17. An answer to this exercise can be found at the end of the teacher's edition.

18. The pH of the water will increase. An acid can be added to lower the pH and correct the problem.

19. A weak base should be used to treat the bite. It will neutralize the acid.

20. Organic compounds should have low melting points, should not dissolve well in water, and should not conduct an electric current in solution.

21. The taste of the soil can help a farmer determine if the soil is acidic or basic. If the soil tastes sour, it is acidic. If the soil tastes bitter, it is basic.

22. A diet containing no lipids is unhealthy because lipids are the major component of cell membranes and are important for storing energy and certain vitamins.

23. B and C

24. A and D

25. A

Reinforcement

A SIMPLE SOLUTION

Acids: taste sour, may be corrosive, react with baking soda to produce carbon dioxide gas, change blue litmus to red, pH less than 7, found in vinegar, excess hydronium ions, found in orange juice, H^+

Bases: taste bitter, may be corrosive, excess hydroxide ions, found in drain cleaner, pH greater than 7, used to make soap, slippery, OH^-, change red litmus to blue, neutralize lakes with low pH

Salts: form from the reaction of a metal and a nonmetal, sodium chloride, formed from a neutralization reaction, used in plasterboard, used to de-ice roads

Critical Thinking

1. Chef Season's bread rises because yeast release carbon dioxide bubbles. The bubbles become trapped in the bread, expanding the dough and causing the bread to rise.

2. Chef Roma uses baking soda and cream of tartar instead of yeast. When baking soda is combined with an acid, it produces carbon dioxide bubbles, causing the bread to rise.

3. a. Because butter is a covalent compound, it does not dissolve well in water. If the butter is combined with the flour first, the water and flour will not mix well.

b. If the flour and water do not mix well, they will not form elastic sheets that trap carbon dioxide. Therefore, the bread will not rise as well or become fluffy.

4. Cream of tartar is an acid. Too much acid will cause the bread to taste sour.

5. Accept all reasonable answers. Sample answer: I think Chef Season will win. Even though her bread may not rise, it will probably taste better than Chef Roma's sour bread.

Section Quizzes

SECTION: IONIC AND COVALENT COMPOUNDS

1. B	**6.** B
2. C	**7.** A
3. D	**8.** B
4. A	**9.** B
5. B	**10.** B

SECTION: ACIDS AND BASES

1. C	**6.** A
2. A	**7.** C
3. B	**8.** A
4. C	**9.** B
5. C	

SECTIONS: SOLUTIONS OF ACIDS AND BASES

1. C	**6.** B
2. D	**7.** D
3. A	**8.** D
4. B	**9.** A
5. B	**10.** D

SECTIONS: ORGANIC COMPOUNDS

1. D	**6.** A
2. E	**7.** D
3. C	**8.** A
4. F	**9.** B
5. B	**10.** C

Chapter Test A

1. C	**8.** B
2. D	**9.** C
3. C	**10.** D
4. A	**11.** G
5. C	**12.** D
6. B	**13.** B
7. C	**14.** F

15. A	**21.** A
16. C	**22.** D
17. H	**23.** B
18. E	**24.** C
19. C	**25.** A
20. B	

Chapter Test B

1. covalent	**8.** A
2. base	**9.** D
3. proteins	**10.** C
4. salt	**11.** C
5. nucleic acid	**12.** D
6. C	**13.** C
7. B	

14. Answers will vary. Sample answer: Any change in the pH of a living thing or its environment will affect its ability to survive. For example, acid rain can change the pH level of a lake and kill fish and other organisms.

15. Answers will vary. Sample answer. The positive and negative ions in an ionic compound are arranged in a three-dimensional crystal lattice. Ionic compounds have strong bonds and high melting points, dissolve easily in water, and can conduct an electric current when dissolved. The bonds between the molecules of covalent compounds are usually weaker than the bonds in ionic compounds. Covalent compounds generally have lower melting points, do not dissolve as well in water, and typically do not conduct an electric current.

16. Answers will vary. Sample answer: Simple carbohydrates are made of a single sugar molecule or a few sugar molecules bonded together. Complex carbohydrates are made of hundreds to thousands of sugar molecules bonded together.

17. Answers will vary. Sample answer: The team would first want to neutralize the acid by adding a weak base. This will react with the acid to form water and a salt, which can be safely cleaned up.

18. The red cabbage juice acted as an indicator. An indicator is a substance that changes color in the presence of an acid or a base.

19. A weak base should be used to treat the bite. It will neutralize the acid.

20. a. hydrocarbons; **b.** unsaturated; **c.** double bond; **d.** triple bond; **e.** aromatic; **f.** saturated; **g.** single bond; **h.** alkane

Chapter Test C

1. C
2. A
3. A
4. A
5. D
6. B
7. D
8. D
9. A
10. C
11. B
12. A
13. D
14. B
15. A
16. D
17. C
18. pH
19. salt
20. neutralization reaction
21. organic compounds
22. biochemicals

Standardized Test Preparation

READING

Passage 1

1. C
2. H
3. D

Passage 2

1. B
2. F
3. A

INTERPRETING GRAPHICS

1. B
2. I
3. C

MATH

1. B
2. I
3. C

Vocabulary Activity

1. hydrocarbons
2. covalent
3. nucleic acids
4. pH
5. lipids
6. salt
7. acid
8. biochemicals
9. base
10. carbohydrates
11. ionic
12. organic
13. proteins
14. litmus
15. amino acids
16. insulin
17. complex
18. indicator
19. four
20. DNA
21. saturated
22. hemoglobin
23. bond

Y	X	B	H	T	A	R	O	T	A	C	I	D	N	I	A
J	C	E	I	P	N	X	A	B	R	M	W	S	O	N	L
A	H	I	L	O	T	E	I	O	B	I	A	E	D	I	T
S	W	L	N	P	C	L	P	N	I	L	S	C	P	I	L
N	S	R	A	A	M	H	A	D	X	A	A	I	N	Y	N
O	D	S	C	G	G	O	E	S	B	R	D	I	D	C	I
B	I	N	K	A	A	R	C	M	B	S	L	M	V	H	B
R	C	I	Z	V	U	U	O	O	I	U	W	N	U	P	O
A	A	E	J	O	E	Y	H	C	S	C	Q	P	H	G	L
C	O	T	F	A	E	Y	O	N	A	L	A	E	T	X	G
O	N	O	V	W	D	V	I	H	H	C	I	L	I	G	O
R	I	R	L	R	A	I	X	Y	F	M	I	T	S	Q	M
D	M	P	A	L	O	J	K	V	K	K	T	D	M	H	E
Y	A	T	E	N	G	L	V	P	B	E	D	U	Q	U	H
H	E	N	I	N	B	D	E	T	A	R	U	T	A	S	S
S	T	C	N	U	C	L	E	I	C	A	C	I	D	S	R

SciLinks Activity

1. Students should draw a pH scale—a line that goes from 1–12. Students should use the websites to find the pH for as many substances as they can (at least 10) and write the name of the substance at the right place on the pH scale. Answers will vary. Common acids include: lemon juice, vinegar, orange juice, carbonated beverages, stomach acid, and battery acid. Common bases include: baking soda, bleach, ammonia, drain cleaner, and soap. Some neutral substances include: water, milk, and hand lotion.

2. Answers will vary. Sample answers: The word *lemon* means "sour." Acids are good conductors of electricity. Acids dissolve metals. For example, tomato sauce may remove the finish from aluminum pans. Strong acids are corrosive and may cause burns. They react with bases to produce carbon dioxide gas. Bases feel soapy or slippery when rubbed with the fingers because they react with oils to dissolve them. They form ions in water and are good conductors of electricity. Concentrated solutions of bases are as corrosive as strong acids and may cause severe burns. Bases react with acids to form neutral substances that cancel out the acidity.

3. Answers will vary. Sample answers: Acids can be used as preservatives to kill bacteria in foods. The fizzing reaction produced by the interaction of acids and bases is used in baking to make cakes rise. Bases are used in the chemical industry to make fertilizer, glass, and cement. They are sometimes added to soil and water to reduce the effects of acid rain. The reaction between acids and bases can be used to treat plant and animal stings. In fire extinguishers, it is used to produce a foam of carbon dioxide gas.

Lesson Plan

Section: Ionic and Covalent Compounds

Pacing

Regular Schedule: **with lab(s):** N/A   **without lab(s):** 1 day

Block Schedule: **with lab(s):** N/A   **without lab(s):** 0.5 day

Objectives

1. Describe the properties of ionic and covalent compounds.

2. Classify compounds as ionic or covalent based on their properties.

National Science Education Standards Covered

UCP 1: Systems, order, and organization

SAI 2: Understandings about scientific inquiry

PS 1a: A substance has characteristic properties, such as density, a boiling point, and solubility, all of which are independent of the amount of the sample. A mixture of substances often can be separated into the original substances using one or more of the characteristic properties.

PS 1b: Substances react chemically in characteristic ways with other substances to form new substances (compounds) with different characteristic properties. In chemical reactions, the total mass is conserved. Substances often are placed in categories or groups if they react in similar ways; metals are an example of such a group.

KEY

SE = Student Edition   **TE** = Teacher's Edition

CRF = Chapter Resource File

FOCUS *(5 minutes)*

_ **Bellringer, TE** Divide students into two groups for an exercise to simulate ionic and covalent bonds.

_ **Bellringer Transparency** Use this transparency as students enter the classroom and find their seats.

MOTIVATE *(10 minutes)*

_ **Demonstration, TE, Observing Crystals** Have students observe salt and sugar crystals shown with a microprojector or projection microscope. (**GENERAL**)

TEACH *(20 minutes)*

_ **Reading Strategy, SE** Have students make a concept map as they read the chapter. (**GENERAL**)

_ **Reading Strategy, Prediction Guide, TE** Have students predict whether certain chemicals are ionic or covalent compounds. (**GENERAL**)

_ **Connection to History, Bonding Theory, TE** Provide students with information about Gilbert N. Lewis. (**ADVANCED**)

_ **Directed Reading A/B, CRF** These worksheets reinforce basic oncepts and vocabulary presented in this lesson. (**BASIC/SPECIAL NEEDS**)

_ **Vocabulary and Section Summary, CRF** Students write definitions of key terms and read a summary of section content. (**GENERAL**)

CLOSE *(10 minutes)*

_ **Reteaching, Chemical Bond Review, TE** Have students review the concepts of ionic bonds and covalent bonds by organizing information into a table. (**BASIC**)

_ **Section Review, SE** Students answers end-of-section vocabulary, key ideas, math and critical thinking questions. (**GENERAL**)

_ **Section Quiz, CRF** Students answer 9 objective questions about ionic and covalent compounds. (**GENERAL**)

_ **Quiz, TE** Students answer 3 questions about ionic and covalent compounds. (**GENERAL**)

_ **Alternative Assessment, Bonding Story, TE** Have students write short stories about the difference between ionic and covalent compounds. (**GENERAL**)

Lesson Plan

Section: Acids and Bases

Pacing

Regular Schedule: **with lab(s):** N/A   **without lab(s):** 1 day

Block Schedule: **with lab(s):** N/A   **without lab(s):** 0.5 day

Objectives

1. Describe the four properties of acids.
2. Identify four uses of acids.
3. Describe four properties of bases.
4. Identify four uses of bases.

National Science Education Standards Covered

UCP 1: Systems, order, and organization

SAI 1: Abilities necessary to do scientific inquiry

SPSP 4: Risks and benefits

PS 1a: A substance has characteristic properties, such as density, a boiling point, and solubility, all of which are independent of the amount of the sample. A mixture of substances often can be separated into the original substances using one or more of the characteristic properties.

PS 1b: Substances react chemically in characteristic ways with other substances to form new substances (compounds) with different characteristic properties. In chemical reactions, the total mass is conserved. Substances often are placed in categories or groups if they react in similar ways; metals is an example of such a group.

KEY

SE = Student Edition   **TE** = Teacher's Edition

CRF = Chapter Resource File

FOCUS *(5 minutes)*

- **Bellringer, TE** Show students a lemon and a tomato and have them suggest other foods whose tanginess may be due to the presence of acids.

- **Bellringer Transparency** Use this transparency as students enter the classroom and find their seats.

MOTIVATE *(10 minutes)*

- **Activity, Tasting a Weak Acid, TE** Have students taste carbonated water and regular water and compare the flavor of both. **(GENERAL)**

TEACH *(20 minutes)*

_ **Demonstration, A Fruit Juice Indicator, TE** Show students how three substances can affect diluted grape juice. (**GENERAL**)

_ **Connection to Biology, SE** Have students research and make a poster describing how acids are used in hair care products. (**GENERAL**)

_ **Activity, Comparing Acids and Bases, TE** Have students make a table comparing the properties of acids and bases as they read. (**BASIC**)

_ **Demonstration, A Base From a Metal, TE** Form a metal oxide by burning magnesium ribbon, then test a solution of the metal oxide in water with litmus paper. (**GENERAL**)

_ **Demonstration, Making Soap, TE** Demonstrate how soap is made using lard and sodium hydroxide solution. (**GENERAL**)

_ **Inclusion Strategies, TE** Have students create a wall web about acids and bases.

_ **Directed Reading A/B, CRF** These worksheets reinforce basic concepts and vocabulary presented in this lesson. (**BASIC/SPECIAL NEEDS**)

_ **Vocabulary and Section Summary, CRF** Students write definitions of key terms and read a summary of section content. (**GENERAL**)

_ **Critical Thinking, CRF** Have the students use their knowledge of acids and bases to predict who will win a baking contest. (**ADVANCED**)

_ **Quick Lab, SE** Have students test various solutions with red and blue litmus paper. (**GENERAL**)

CLOSE *(10 minutes)*

_ **Reteaching, Acids and Bases Review, TE** Have students make an outline of this section then use students' outlines to create a study guide. (**BASIC**)

_ **Section Review, SE** Students answers end-of-section vocabulary, key ideas, math and critical thinking questions. (**GENERAL**)

_ **Homework, Soapmaking, TE** Have students research soap making and write a short report. (**GENERAL**)

_ **Section Quiz, CRF** Students answer 9 objective questions about acids and bases. (**GENERAL**)

_ **Quiz, TE** Students answer 2 questions about acids and bases. (**GENERAL**)

_ **Alternative Assessment, TE** Have students create a poster board display of acids and bases. (**GENERAL**)

Lesson Plan

Section: Solutions of Acids and Bases

Pacing

Regular Schedule: **with lab(s):** 2 days   **without lab(s):** 1 day

Block Schedule: **with lab(s):** 1 day   **without lab(s):** 0.5 day

Objectives

1. Explain the difference between strong acids and bases and weak acids and bases.
2. Identify acids and bases by using the pH scale.
3. Describe the formation and uses of salt.

National Science Education Standards Covered

UCP 1: Systems, order, and organization

UCP 2: Evidence, models, and explanation

UCP 4: Evolution and equilibrium

SAI 1: Abilities necessary to do scientific inquiry

ST 2: Understandings about science and technology

SPSP 1: Personal health

SPSP 3: Natural hazards

PS 1b: Substances react chemically in characteristic ways with other substances to form new substances (compounds) with different characteristic properties. In chemical reactions, the total mass is conserved. Substances often are placed in categories or groups if they react in similar ways; metals are an example of such a group.

KEY

SE = Student Edition   **TE** = Teacher's Edition
CRF = Chapter Resource File

FOCUS *(5 minutes)*

- **Bellringer, TE** Bring in product labels from vinegar products, citrus products, soaps, cleaning agents, and other household products. Ask students to work in pairs and identify which ingredients are acids and which are bases.

- **Bellringer Transparency** Use this transparency as students enter the classroom and find their seats.

MOTIVATE *(10 minutes)*

_ **Discussion, TE** Demonstrate equal concentrations of a strong and a weak acid. **(GENERAL)**

_ **Reading Strategy, SE** Have students write questions as they read the section, then form a small group and discuss the questions. **(GENERAL)**

TEACH *(65 minutes)*

_ **Connection Activity, Math, pH Scale, TE** Have students calculate pH using increments on the pH scale. **(GENERAL)**

_ **Chapter Lab, Cabbage Patch Indicators, SE** Students make a natural acid-base indicator solution and determine the pH of common substances. **(GENERAL)**

_ **Datasheet for Chapter Lab, Cabbage Patch Indicators, CRF** Students use the datasheet to complete the Chapter Lab. **(GENERAL)**

_ **Directed Reading A/B, CRF** These worksheets reinforce basic concepts and vocabulary presented in this lesson. **(BASIC/SPECIAL NEEDS)**

_ **Vocabulary and Section Summary, CRF** Students write definitions of key terms and read a summary of section content. **(GENERAL)**

_ **Reinforcement, CRF** This worksheet reinforces key concepts in the chapter. **(BASIC)**

_ **SciLinks Activity, Acids and Bases, SciLinks code HSM0013, CRF** Students research Internet resources related to acids and bases. **(GENERAL)**

_ **Quick Lab, SE** Have students test vinegar and an antacid tablet with red and blue litmus paper. **(GENERAL)**

_ **Teaching Transparency, pH values of Common Materials** Use this graphic to show students more about how the pH scale works.

CLOSE *(10 minutes)*

_ **Section Review, SE** Students answer end-of-section vocabulary, key ideas, math and critical thinking questions. **(GENERAL)**

_ **Homework, TE** Have students research the effect of acid precipitation on various structures, and create a poster describing their findings. **(GENERAL)**

_ **Section Quiz, CRF** Students answer 10 objective questions about solutions of acids and bases. **(GENERAL)**

_ **Quiz, TE** Students answer 3 questions about solutions of acids and bases. **(GENERAL)**

_ **Alternative Assessment, TE** Have students make a concept map of key ideas in the section. **(GENERAL)**

Lesson Plan

Section: Organic Compounds

Pacing

Regular Schedule:	**with lab(s):** N/A	**without lab(s):** 1 day
Block Schedule:	**with lab(s):** N/A	**without lab(s):** 0.5 day

Objectives

1. Explain why so many organic compounds are possible.

2. Identify and describe saturated, unsaturated, and aromatic hydrocarbons.

3. Describe the characteristics of carbohydrates, lipids, proteins, and nucleic acids and their functions in the body.

National Science Education Standards Covered

UCP 1: Systems, order, and organization

SAI 1: Abilities necessary to do scientific inquiry

ST 2: Understandings about science and technology

SPSP 1: Personal health

PS 1a: A substance has characteristic properties, such as density, a boiling point, and solubility, all of which are independent of the amount of the sample. A mixture of substances often can be separated into the original substances using one or more of the characteristic properties.

PS 1b: Substances react chemically in characteristic ways with other substances to form new substances (compounds) with different characteristic properties. In chemical reactions, the total mass is conserved. Substances often are placed in categories or groups if they react in similar ways; metals is an example of such a group.

PS 1c: Chemical elements do not break down during normal laboratory reactions involving such treatments as heating, exposure to electric current, or reaction with acids. There are more than 100 known elements that combine in a multitude of ways to produce compounds, which account for the living and nonliving substances that we encounter.

KEY

SE = Student Edition   **TE** = Teacher's Edition
CRF = Chapter Resource File

FOCUS (*5 minutes*)

_ **Bellringer, TE** Ask students to list as many items containing carbon as they can think of.

_ **Bellringer Transparency** Use this transparency as students enter the classroom and find their seats.

MOTIVATE *(10 minutes)*

_ **Discussion, TE** Discuss with students how vegetarians can receive sufficient protein. (**GENERAL**)

_ **Reading Strategy, SE** Have students read the section silently, form in pairs and summarize the material. (**GENERAL**)

TEACH *(20 minutes)*

_ **Activity, Modeling Hydrocarbons, TE** Have students use two different colors of clay and toothpicks to make models of an alkane, an alkene, and an alkyne. (**GENERAL**)

_ **Connection Activity, Math, Chemical Formulas, TE** Have students analyze formulas for hydrocarbons and discuss the relationships between the formulas. (**GENERAL**)

_ **Directed Reading A/B, CRF** These worksheets reinforce basic concepts and vocabulary presented in this lesson. (**BASIC/SPECIAL NEEDS**)

_ **Vocabulary and Section Summary, CRF** Students write definitions of key terms and read a summary of section content. (**GENERAL**)

_ **Quick Lab, SE** Have the students estimate the carbohydrate and fat content of four empty food packages and then compare with the Nutrition Facts labels. (**GENERAL**)

_ **Teaching Transparency, Structural Formulas** Use this overhead to show the structure of some organic compounds.

_ **Teaching Transparency, Link to Life Science: Phospholipid Molecule and Cell Membrane** Use this overhead to show how lipids help form cell walls.

_ **Guided Practice, Nutrition Labels, TE** Have students find carbohydrate, lipid and protein content on different food labels. (**GENERAL**)

_ **Demonstration, Lipids and Water, TE** Show students how three different lipids behave when added to water. (**GENERAL**)

_ **Activity, DNA, TE** Have students research how DNA stores the information the cell needs for making proteins, then write a report. (**ADVANCED**)

CLOSE *(10 minutes)*

_ **Section Review, SE** Students answers end-of-section vocabulary, key ideas, critical thinking, and interpreting graphics questions. (**GENERAL**)

_ **Section Quiz, CRF** Students answer 10 objective questions about organic compounds. (**GENERAL**)

_ **Quiz, TE** Students answer 3 basic questions about organic compounds. (**GENERAL**)

_ **Alternative Assessment, Building a Model, TE** Have students create a model of a DNA molecule, then display models in class. (**GENERAL**)

Lesson Plan

End of Chapter Review and Assessment

Pacing

Regular Schedule: **with lab(s):** N/A   **without lab(s):** 2 days

Block Schedule: **with lab(s):** N/A   **without lab(s):** 1 day

---

KEY

SE = Student Edition   **TE** = Teacher's Edition

CRF = Chapter Resource File

- **Chapter Review, SE** Students answer end-of-chapter vocabulary, key ideas, critical thinking, and graphics questions. (**GENERAL**)

- **Vocabulary Activity, CRF** Students review chapter vocabulary terms by completing a puzzle. (**GENERAL**)

- **Concept Mapping Transparency** Use this graphic to help students review key concepts.

- **Chapter Test A/B/C, CRF** Assign questions from the appropriate test for chapter assessment. (**GENERAL/ADVANCED/SPECIAL NEEDS**)

- **Performance-Based Assessment, CRF** Assign this activity for a general level assessment of the chapter. (**GENERAL**)

- **Standardized Test Preparation, SE** Students answer reading comprehension, math, and interpreting graphics questions in the format of a standardized test. (**GENERAL**)

- **Test Generator, One-Stop Planner** Create a customized homework assignment, quiz, or test using the HRW Test Generator Program.

- **CNN Video, CNN Presents Science in the News: Science, Technology & Society,** Segment 3, "Flavor Cells"

- **CNN Video, CNN Presents Science in the News: Scientists in Action,** Segment 22, "Creating a Coat of Armor"

Holt Science and Technology   **119**   Chemical Compounds

MULTIPLE CHOICE

1. If it is brittle, dissolves easily in water, has a high melting point and conducts electric current it is a(n)
   a. valence electron.
   b. ionic compound.
   c. covalent compound.
   d. sugar.

   Answer: B   Difficulty: 1   Section: 1   Objective: 1

2. Which compound has the weaker chemical bond?
   a. ionic
   b. covalent
   c. metallic
   d. electric

   Answer: B   Difficulty: 1   Section: 1   Objective: 1

3. When a metal reacts with a nonmetal it makes
   a. an ionic compound.
   b. a covalent compound.
   c. a low melting point.
   d. water molecules.

   Answer: A   Difficulty: 1   Section: 1   Objective: 2

4. Most covalent compounds
   a. dissolve in water.
   b. don't dissolve in water.
   c. mix with water.
   d. are positively charged in water.

   Answer: B   Difficulty: 1   Section: 1   Objective: 1

5. Sugar is a covalent compound that dissolves in water but does not form ions, so it
   a. conducts electric current.
   b. does not conduct electric current.
   c. is negatively charged.
   d. is not a compound.

   Answer: B   Difficulty: 1   Section: 1   Objective: 1

6. Covalent compounds have
   a. high melting points.
   b. low melting points.
   c. no melting point.
   d. strong bonds.

   Answer: B   Difficulty: 1   Section: 1   Objective: 1

7. What substances can acids react with to produce hydrogen gas?
   a. water
   b. sugars
   c. metals
   d. poisons

   Answer: C   Difficulty: 1   Section: 2   Objective: 1

8. Acids conduct electric current by forming
   a. hydrochloric acids.
   b. hydrogen gases.
   c. hydronium ions.
   d. hydroxide ions.

   Answer: C   Difficulty: 1   Section: 2   Objective: 1

9. Acids have a
   a. sour taste.
   b. bitter taste.
   c. slippery feel.
   d. soapy feel.

   Answer: A   Difficulty: 1   Section: 2   Objective: 1

10. Bases have a
    a. sour taste.
    b. sweet taste.
    c. slippery feel.
    d. mild taste.

    Answer: C   Difficulty: 1   Section: 2   Objective: 3

11. When a base is added to red litmus paper, the indicator turns
    a. blue.
    b. red.
    c. purple.
    d. orange.

    Answer: A   Difficulty: 1   Section: 2   Objective: 3

12. If a cleaning product includes ammonia as an ingredient, it probably is made from a(n)
    a. acid.
    b. base.
    c. indicator.
    d. powder.
    Answer: B   Difficulty: 1   Section: 2   Objective: 4

13. When all the molecules of an acid break apart in water, the solution is called a
    a. weak acid.
    b. strong acid.
    c. weak base.
    d. strong base.
    Answer: B   Difficulty: 1   Section: 3   Objective: 1

14. Citric acid is a weak acid, so only a few molecules would break apart when
    a. it comes in contact with air.
    b. it dissolves in water.
    c. it neutralizes.
    d. it is forming.
    Answer: B   Difficulty: 1   Section: 3   Objective: 1

15. When acids and bases come in contact with each other, they
    a. explode.
    b. become bitter.
    c. make hydroxide.
    d. neutralize each other.
    Answer: D   Difficulty: 1   Section: 3   Objective: 3

16. One way to test pH is to use a strip of paper that has several
    a. hydronium ions.
    b. bases.
    c. acids.
    d. indicators.
    Answer: D   Difficulty: 1   Section: 3   Objective: 2

17. A neutral solution has a pH of
    a. 7.
    b. 11.
    c. 3.
    d. 1.
    Answer: A   Difficulty: 1   Section: 3   Objective: 2

18. Sodium chloride, sodium nitrate and calcium sulfate are all
    a. sugars.
    b. hydroniums.
    c. indicators.
    d. salts.
    Answer: D   Difficulty: 1   Section: 3   Objective: 3

19. How many atoms can a carbon atom make bonds with?
    a. one
    b. two
    c. three
    d. four
    Answer: D   Difficulty: 1   Section: 4   Objective: 1

20. Which hydrocarbon contains only single bonds between carbon atoms?
    a. saturated
    b. unsaturated
    c. aromatic
    d. inorganic
    Answer: A   Difficulty: 1   Section: 4   Objective: 2

21. Carbohydrates, lipids, proteins and nucleic acids are all
    a. hydrocarbons
    b. biochemicals
    c. fats
    d. plants
    Answer: B   Difficulty: 1   Section: 4   Objective: 3

22. What are aromatic hydrocarbons based on?
    a. water
    b. alkenes
    c. benzene
    d. lipids
    Answer: C   Difficulty: 1   Section: 4   Objective: 2

23. Brittleness and a high melting point are two properties of
    a. covalent compounds.
    b. organic compounds.
    c. ionic compounds.
    d. protein compounds.
    Answer: C   Difficulty: 1   Section: 1   Objective: 1

24. What kind of compound rarely dissolves in water?
    a. ionic
    b. organic
    c. protein
    d. covalent
    Answer: D   Difficulty: 1   Section: 1   Objective: 1

25. What substance has a sour taste and produces hydrogen gas when it reacts with some metals?
    a. base
    b. organic compound
    c. acid
    d. indicator
    Answer: C   Difficulty: 1   Section: 2   Objective: 1

26. This substance has a bitter taste and slippery feel.
    a. base
    b. organic compound
    c. acid
    d. indicator
    Answer: A   Difficulty: 1   Section: 2   Objective: 3

27. If almost all the molecules of an acid break apart when dissolved in water, the acid is
    a. weak.
    b. neutral.
    c. strong.
    d. sour.
    Answer: C   Difficulty: 1   Section: 3   Objective: 1

28. A substance that is rated 7 on the pH scale is considered
    a. basic.
    b. neutral.
    c. weak.
    d. acidic.
    Answer: B   Difficulty: 1   Section: 3   Objective: 2

29. When an acid and a base neutralize each other, what remains?
    a. a weak acid and base
    b. a strong acid and base
    c. water and a salt.
    d. a lipid and a protein
    Answer: C   Difficulty: 1   Section: 3   Objective: 3

30. Over 90% of compounds are what type?
    a. ionic
    b. organic
    c. inorganic
    d. covalent
    Answer: B   Difficulty: 1   Section: 4   Objective: 1

31. What type of hydrocarbon has double and triple bonds between carbon atoms?
    a. saturated
    b. aromatic
    c. unsaturated
    d. neutral
    Answer: C   Difficulty: 1   Section: 4   Objective: 2

32. Biochemicals composed of one or more simple sugar molecules are called
    a. proteins.
    b. nucleic acids.
    c. lipids.
    d. carbohydrates.
    Answer: D   Difficulty: 1   Section: 4   Objective: 3

33. Hemoglobin, which carries oxygen in the blood, is a
    a. carbohydrate.
    b. lipid.
    c. protein.
    d. nucleic acid.
    Answer: C   Difficulty: 1   Section: 4   Objective: 3

34. Which of the following make up over 90% of all known compounds?
    a. ionic compounds
    b. organic compounds
    c. basic compounds
    d. aromatic compounds
    Answer: B   Difficulty: 1   Section: 4   Objective: 1

35. Vitamins that do not dissolve in water are stored in
    a. lipids.
    b. proteins.
    c. carbohydrates.
    d. nucleic acids.
    Answer: A   Difficulty: 1   Section: 4   Objective: 3

36. The walls of cell membranes are made of what kind of biochemical?
    a. protein
    b. cellulose
    c. cholesterol
    d. lipid
    Answer: D   Difficulty: 1   Section: 4   Objective: 3

37. Glucose is a
    a. wax.
    b. starch
    c. simple carbohydrate.
    d. complex carbohydrate.
    Answer: C   Difficulty: 1   Section: 4   Objective: 3

38. Which of the following, in equal concentrations, has the lowest pH?
    a. salt
    b. strong base
    c. strong acid
    d. a weak acid
    Answer: C   Difficulty: 1   Section: 3   Objective: 2

39. Which of these statements about proteins is incorrect?
    a. Certain proteins provide structural support for cells.
    b. Proteins are involved in the transport of molecules across membranes.
    c. The function of a protein depends on its shape.
    d. Nucleic acids are the building blocks of proteins.
    Answer: D   Difficulty: 2   Section: 4   Objective: 3

40. Which of the following is an ionic compound?
    a. glucose
    b. water
    c. sodium chloride
    d. vegetable oil
    Answer: C   Difficulty: 1   Section: 1   Objective: 2

41. What compounds are brittle and have high melting points?
    a. covalent
    b. organic
    c. ionic
    d. nucleic
    Answer: C   Difficulty: 1   Section: 1   Objective: 1

42. What force of attraction holds atoms or ions together?
    a. chemical bond
    b. chemical reaction
    c. nucleic acid
    d. neutralization
    Answer: A   Difficulty: 1   Section: 1   Objective: 1

43. Why should you NEVER taste or touch an unknown acid?
    a. It could be corrosive.
    b. It could be slippery.
    c. It could smell bad.
    d. It could bite you.
    Answer: A   Difficulty: 1   Section: 2   Objective: 1

44. What do foods that taste sour usually contain?
    a. acid
    b. base
    c. indicator
    d. water
    Answer: A   Difficulty: 1   Section: 2   Objective: 1

45. What compound used in cleaners feels slippery?
    a. acid
    b. sugar
    c. salt
    d. base
    Answer: D   Difficulty: 1   Section: 2   Objective: 3

46. In what type of solution do all the molecules of an acid break apart in water?
    a. weak acid
    b. strong acid
    c. medium acid
    d. neutral
    Answer: B   Difficulty: 1   Section: 3   Objective: 1

47. What is left when a base and an acid neutralize?
    a. hydrochloric acid
    b. pH
    c. hydronium ions
    d. water and a salt
    Answer: D   Difficulty: 1   Section: 3   Objective: 3

48. What kind of melting point do ionic compounds have?
    a. low
    b. neutral
    c. strong
    d. high
    Answer: D   Difficulty: 1   Section: 1   Objective: 1

49. What type of acid is used to make plastics?
    a. nitric
    b. hydrochloric
    c. sulfuric
    d. carbonic
    Answer: A   Difficulty: 1   Section: 2   Objective: 2

50. A substance is made of carbon and hydrogen. The four bonds it shares with four other atoms are very strong. It is
    a. an aromatic hydrocarbon.
    b. an alkene.
    c. an alkane.
    d. an alkyne.
    Answer: C   Difficulty: 3   Section: 4   Objective: 2

51. A factory that has not followed pollution control standards has been operating in an area that did not have such a factory before. Plants that used to grow well are not doing as well. Fish in a nearby river are dying at a higher rate than usual. Why?
    a. Pollution from the factory is getting into the rain, which is making the pH levels in the soil and water rise.
    b. It hasn't rained enough, and the plants aren't getting enough water.
    c. The factory has increased the temperature in the area.
    d. Pollution from the factory is getting into rain, which is making pH levels in the soil and water become lower.
    Answer: D   Difficulty: 2   Section: 3   Objective: 2

52. If you know that Zn stands for Zinc and 2HCl stands for hydrochloric acid, you can tell what this equation represents:
    $2HCl + Zn \longrightarrow H_2 + ZnCl_2$
    a. a weak base reacting with a strong acid
    b. an acid reacting with a metal to produce hydrogen gas
    c. a salt being formed from ions
    d. an indicator changing color to show that something is an acid
    Answer: B   Difficulty: 2   Section: 2   Objective: 1

53. What property of the ionic compound does the crystal lattice shape contribute to?
    a. solubility
    b. conductivity of electric current
    c. changing the color of indicators
    d. brittleness
    Answer: D   Difficulty: 2   Section: 1   Objective: 1

54. Since you know that most calcium hydroxide molecules break apart in water, decide which number on a pH scale would the water the cement-laying tools were washed in be found near?
    a. 3
    b. 7
    c. 10
    d. 8
    Answer: C   Difficulty: 3   Section: 3   Objective: 2

55. Of the following words, which is a broad category that includes the other three?
    a. amino acids
    b. biochemicals
    c. organic compounds
    d. proteins
    Answer: C   Difficulty: 2   Section: 4   Objective: 1

COMPLETION

Use the terms from the following list to complete the sentences below.

proteins
ionic
salt
biochemical

base
nucleic acid
covalent
lipids

56. When electrons are shared between atoms of two different elements
_______________ compounds are formed.
Answer: covalent   Difficulty: 1   Section: 1   Objective: 1

57. Limewater with a pH of 10.5 is a(n) _______________.
Answer: base   Difficulty: 1   Section: 3   Objective: 2

58. Enzymes are _______________ that increase the rate of chemical reactions in
biological systems.
Answer: proteins   Difficulty: 1   Section: 4   Objective: 3

59. When an acid neutralizes a base, a(n) _______________ is formed.
Answer: salt   Difficulty: 1   Section: 3   Objective: 3

60. RNA is a(n) _______________ that plays an active role in protein synthesis.
Answer: nucleic acid   Difficulty: 1   Section: 4   Objective: 3

Use the terms from the following list to complete the sentences below.

pH
salt

biochemicals
neutralization reaction

61. A value used to express acidity or alkalinity is called _______________.
Answer: pH   Difficulty: 1   Section: 3   Objective: 2

62. When an acid neutralizes a base, a(n)_______________ and water are made.
Answer: salt   Difficulty: 1   Section: 3   Objective: 3

63. Organic compounds made by living things are called _______________.
Answer: biochemicals
Difficulty: 1   Section: 4   Objective: 3

64. The reaction between acids and bases is called a(n) _______________.
Answer: neutralization reaction
Difficulty: 1   Section: 3   Objective: 3

Use the terms from the following list to complete the sentences below.

brittleness
solubility

melting point
electrical conductivity

65. When you pour a liquid into water and the liquid rises to the top to float on the water,
you are demonstrating the reason _______________ is not a property of most
covalent compounds.
Answer: solubility
Difficulty: 2   Section: 1   Objective: 2

66. Magnesium oxide provides an example of the _______________ property of ionic
compounds, because it changes to a liquid at 2800 degrees Celsius.
Answer: melting point
Difficulty: 2   Section: 1   Objective: 2

67. Ionic compounds have the property of _________________ because of their crystal lattice shape.
   Answer: brittleness
   Difficulty: 2   Section: 1   Objective: 1

68. More ionic compounds than covalent compounds have the property of _________________ because most covalent compounds do not become charged or form ions when they dissolve in water.
   Answer: electrical conductivity
   Difficulty: 2   Section: 1   Objective: 1

Use the terms from the following list to complete the sentences below.

flavor   indicator
hydrogen gas   electric current

69. If it weren't dangerous to taste them, a good test of whether a substance would be a acid or base would be the _________________.
   Answer: flavor
   Difficulty: 1   Section: 2   Objective: 1

70. One property that acids and bases share is the fact that acids form hydronium ions and bases form hydroxide ions as they dissolve in water, so _________________ can move through a liquid they have dissolved in.
   Answer: electric current
   Difficulty: 2   Section: 2   Objectives: 1, 3

71. Acids can create _________________ by reacting with metals.
   Answer: hydrogen gas
   Difficulty: 1   Section: 2   Objective: 1

72. Litmus is a(n) _________________ because if red litmus comes in contact with a base it will turn blue.
   Answer: indicator   Difficulty: 1   Section: 2   Objective: 3

Use the terms from the following list to complete the sentences below.

acids   bases
reaction   salt

73. All of the terms in the list have to do with the _________________ when H^+ ions meet OH^- ions and form water.
   Answer: reaction   Difficulty: 2   Section: 2   Objective: 3

74. Strong _________________ include sulfuric, nitric and hydrochloric; weak ones include acetic, citric and carbonic.
   Answer: acids   Difficulty: 1   Section: 3   Objective: 1

75. An antacid is an example of weak _________________, such as ammonium hydroxide and aluminum hydroxide.
   Answer: bases   Difficulty: 1   Section: 3   Objective: 1

76. After H^+ ions meet OH^- ions and any water created evaporates, any other ions present join in an ionic compound called a _________________.
   Answer: salt   Difficulty: 2   Section: 3   Objective: 3

Use the terms from the following list to complete the sentences below.

carbohydrates   lipids
proteins   nucleic acids

77. If your hair is curly, you're tall and you have brown eyes, it is because of the information in your _____________________.
   Answer: nucleic acids
                  Difficulty: 2   Section: 4   Objective: 3

78. There are more _____________________ than any of the other three categories of biochemicals, which is good because they regulate many functions of the body.
   Answer: proteins   Difficulty: 2   Section: 4   Objective: 3

79. The reason celery stalks stand up straight is the _____________________ which provide the structure.
   Answer: carbohydrates
                  Difficulty: 1   Section: 4   Objective: 3

80. Vegetables have them, cell walls have them, people need some _____________________.
   Answer: lipids   Difficulty: 2   Section: 4   Objective: 3

SHORT ANSWER

81. In what ways do changes in pH affect the environment and living things?
   Answer:
   Answers will vary. Sample answer: Any change in the pH of a living thing or its environment will affect its ability to survive. For example, acid rain can change the pH level of a lake and kill fish and other organisms.
   Difficulty: 1   Section: 3   Objective: 2

82. How are ionic compounds different from covalent compounds?
   Answer:
   Answers will vary. Sample answer. The positive and negative ions in an ionic compound are arranged in a three-dimensional crystal lattice. Ionic compounds have strong bonds and high melting points, dissolve easily in water, and can conduct an electric current when dissolved. The bonds between the molecules of covalent compounds are usually weaker than the bonds in ionic compounds. Covalent compounds generally have lower melting points, do not dissolve as well in water, and typically do not conduct an electric current.
   Difficulty: 1   Section: 1   Objective: 1

83. Describe the main difference between simple and complex carbohydrates.
   Answer:
   Answers will vary. Sample answer: Simple carbohydrates are made of a single sugar molecule or a few sugar molecules bonded together. Complex carbohydrates are made of hundreds to thousands of sugar molecules bonded together.
   Difficulty: 2   Section: 4   Objective: 3

84. How are ionic compounds formed?
   Answer:
   by the transfer of electrons from metal atoms to nonmetal atoms
   Difficulty: 1   Section: 1   Objective: 1

85. Give two examples of covalent compounds.
   Answer:
   Answers will vary. Sample answer: (2 of these): sugar, water, carbon dioxide.
   Difficulty: 2   Section: 1   Objective: 2

86. Potassium chloride is a crystalline solid that has a melting point of 770°C. Is it more likely to be ionic or covalent?

     Answer: ionic   Difficulty: 2   Section: 1   Objective: 2

87. Classify each of the following compounds as acidic or a basic: soap, vinegar, bleach, baking soda, ammonia, lemonade, magnesium hydroxide.

     Answer:
        acidic: vinegar, lemonade; basic: soap, bleach, ammonia, magnesium hydroxide
     Difficulty: 2   Section: 2   Objective: 2, 4

88. When an acid is added to water, does the number of hydronium ions increase or decrease?

     Answer: increase   Difficulty: 2   Section: 2   Objective: 1

89. Describe the reaction of a base with red litmus paper.

     Answer:
        Red litmus paper turns blue when it touches a base.
     Difficulty: 1   Section: 2   Objective: 3

90. Is the compound H_3PO_4 an acid or a base? How do you know?

     Answer:
        It is an acid because it will form hydrogen ions.
     Difficulty: 2   Section: 3   Objective: 1

91. Would you expect the pH of a sample of acid rain to be 4 or 9? Why?

     Answer:
        4, because it is acidic.
     Difficulty: 2   Section: 3   Objective: 2

92. What products would form when hydrochloric acid, HCl, and sodium hydroxide, NaOH, react?

     Answer:
        The products would be water and the salt sodium chloride.
     Difficulty: 3   Section: 3   Objective: 3

93. How many bonds does carbon form?

     Answer: 4   Difficulty: 1   Section: 4   Objective: 1

94. Name four kinds of biochemicals

     Answer:
        proteins, nucleic acids, carbohydrates and lipids
     Difficulty: 1   Section: 4   Objective: 3

95. A glass with clear bubbly liquid is on the counter. You're not sure if it's a carbonated drink or water someone has dissolved antacid in it. How could you tell without tasting the liquid?

     Answer:
        Test it with litmus paper. If a blue litmus paper turns red, it is probably the carbonated drink, which has acid. If a red litmus paper turns blue, it is probably water with antacid dissolved in it.
     Difficulty: 3   Section: 3   Objective: 1

96. Explain the difference between the concentration of a base and the strength of a base.

     Answer:
        the concentration means how much base there is. The strength of the base is what percentage of the molecules break down to produce hydroxide ions when the base is dissolved in water.
     Difficulty: 3   Section: 3   Objective: 1

MATCHING

    a. covalent compound   c. ionic compound
    b. chemical bond   d. valence electrons

97. _____ the force of attraction that holds atoms or ions together
    Answer: B   Difficulty: 1   Section: 1   Objective: 1

98. _____ compound made of oppositely charged ions
    Answer: C   Difficulty: 1   Section: 1   Objective: 1

99. _____ located in the outermost energy level of an atom; their behavior determines what kind of compound is formed
    Answer: D   Difficulty: 1   Section: 1   Objective: 1

100. _____ a chemical compound formed by the sharing of electrons
    Answer: A   Difficulty: 1   Section: 1   Objective: 1

    a. indicator   c. acid
    b. base

101. _____ any compound that increases the number of hydronium ions when dissolved in water
    Answer: C   Difficulty: 1   Section: 2   Objective: 1

102. _____ a compound that can reversibly change color depending on conditions such as pH
    Answer: A   Difficulty: 1   Section: 2   Objective: 1, 3

103. _____ any compound that increases the number of hydroxide ions when dissolved in water
    Answer: B   Difficulty: 1   Section: 2   Objective: 3

    a. neutralization reaction   c. pH
    b. hydronium ion concentration   d. salt

104. _____ a value used to express the acidity or alkalinity (basicity) of a system
    Answer: C   Difficulty: 1   Section: 3   Objective: 2

105. _____ an ionic compound formed from the positive ion of a base and the negative ion of an acid when they combine
    Answer: D   Difficulty: 1   Section: 3   Objective: 3

106. _____ the reaction of an acid and a base to form a neutral solution of water and a salt
    Answer: A   Difficulty: 1   Section: 3   Objective: 3

107. _____ measured by pH
    Answer: B   Difficulty: 1   Section: 3   Objective: 2

    a. nucleic acid   d. organic compound
    b. protein   e. hydrocarbon
    c. carbohydrate   f. lipid

108. _____ a covalently bonded compound that has carbon-based molecules
    Answer: D   Difficulty: 1   Section: 4   Objective: 1

109. _____ an organic compound composed only of carbon and hydrogen
    Answer: E   Difficulty: 1   Section: 4   Objective: 2

110. _____ a class of energy-giving nutrients that includes sugars, starches and fiber
    Answer: C   Difficulty: 1   Section: 4   Objective: 3

111. _____ a type of biochemical that does not dissolve in water, includes fats and steroids
    Answer: F   Difficulty: 1   Section: 4   Objective: 3

112. _____ an organic compound that is made of one or more chains of amino acids and is in all cells
    Answer: B   Difficulty: 1   Section: 4   Objective: 3

113. _____ an organic compound, either RNA or DNA, whose molecules are made up of one or two chains of nucleotides
    Answer: A   Difficulty: 1   Section: 4   Objective: 3

a. hydrocarbon
b. chemical bond
c. indicator
d. salt

e. pH
f. lipid
g. covalent compound
h. nucleic acid

114. _____ a chemical compound formed by the sharing of electrons
    Answer: G   Difficulty: 1   Section: 1   Objective: 1
115. _____ an ionic compound formed from the positive ion of a base and the negative ion of an acid
    Answer: D   Difficulty: 1   Section: 3   Objective: 3
116. _____ the force of attraction that holds atoms or ions together
    Answer: B   Difficulty: 1   Section: 1   Objective: 1
117. _____ a type of biochemical that does not dissolve in water
    Answer: F   Difficulty: 1   Section: 4   Objective: 3
118. _____ an organic compound that contains only carbon and hydrogen
    Answer: A   Difficulty: 1   Section: 4   Objective: 2
119. _____ a compound that can change color depending on the pH of the solution
    Answer: C   Difficulty: 1   Section: 2   Objective: 1, 3
120. _____ an organic compound that carries genetic information
    Answer: H   Difficulty: 1   Section: 4   Objective: 3
121. _____ a value that is used to express the acidity or basicity (alkalinity) of a system
    Answer: E   Difficulty: 1   Section: 3   Objective: 2

a. carbohydrates
b. lipids

c. proteins
d. nucleic acids

122. _____ composed of amino acids
    Answer: C   Difficulty: 1   Section: 4   Objective: 3
123. _____ include fats, oils and waves
    Answer: B   Difficulty: 1   Section: 4   Objective: 3
124. _____ include sugars, starches and fiber
    Answer: A   Difficulty: 1   Section: 4   Objective: 3
125. _____ sometimes called the blueprints of life
    Answer: D   Difficulty: 1   Section: 4   Objective: 3

a. neutralization reaction
b. acid rain

c. sodium nitrate

126. _____ may kill fish and other organisms
    Answer: B   Difficulty: 1   Section: 3   Objective: 1
127 _____ used to preserve food
    Answer: C   Difficulty: 1   Section: 3   Objective: 3
128. _____ occurs when acids and bases react
    Answer: A   Difficulty: 1   Section: 3   Objective: 3

a. proteins
b. lipids

c. carbohydrates
d. nucleic acid

129. _____ made of sugar molecules
    Answer: C   Difficulty: 1   Section: 4   Objective: 3
130. _____ do not dissolve in water
    Answer: B   Difficulty: 1   Section: 4   Objective: 3
131. _____ made of amino acids
    Answer: A   Difficulty: 1   Section: 4   Objective: 3
132. _____ store genetic information
    Answer: D   Difficulty: 1   Section: 4   Objective: 3

a. hydrocarbons

b. ionic compounds

c. covalent compounds

d. indicators

133. ____ formed by a metal and a nonmetal

Answer: B   Difficulty: 1   Section: 1   Objective: 1

134. ____ can be saturated or unsaturated

Answer: A   Difficulty: 1   Section: 4   Objective: 2

135. ____ change color depending on conditions such as pH

Answer: D   Difficulty: 1   Section: 2   Objective: 1, 3

136. ____ formed by atoms that share an electron

Answer: C   Difficulty: 1   Section: 1   Objective: 1

ESSAY

137. How could a spill-response team use neutralization to safely clean up a large spill of hydrochloric acid?

Answer:

Answers will vary. Sample answer: The team would first want to neutralize the acid by adding a weak base. This will react with the acid to form water and a salt, which can be safely cleaned up.

Difficulty: 2   Section: 3   Objective: 3

138. A student added a few drops of lemon juice to a glass of red cabbage juice. The lemon juice turned the cabbage juice pink. When the student added a few drops of liquid soap to the red cabbage juice, the juice turned green. What function did the red cabbage juice serve? Explain.

Answer:

The red cabbage juice acted as an indicator. An indicator is a substance that changes color in the presence of an acid or a base.

Difficulty: 2   Section: 2   Objective: 1, 3

139. Many insects, such as fire ants, inject formic acid, a weak acid, when they bite or sting. What kind of compound should be used to treat this kind of bite?

Answer:

A weak base should be used to treat the bite. It will neutralize the acid.

Difficulty: 2   Section: 3   Objective: 3

140. What is the role of valence electrons in forming ionic or covalent compounds?

Answer:

the behavior of valence electrons determines whether the substance is an ionic compound or a covalent compound. If atoms trade a molecule, you have an ionic compound. If atoms share an electron with another compound, that is a covalent molecule.

Difficulty: 3   Section: 1   Objective: 1

INTERPRETING GRAPHICS

141. Use the following terms to complete the concept map below:

saturated
aromatic
double bond
hydrocarbons

single bond
triple bond
unsaturated
alkane

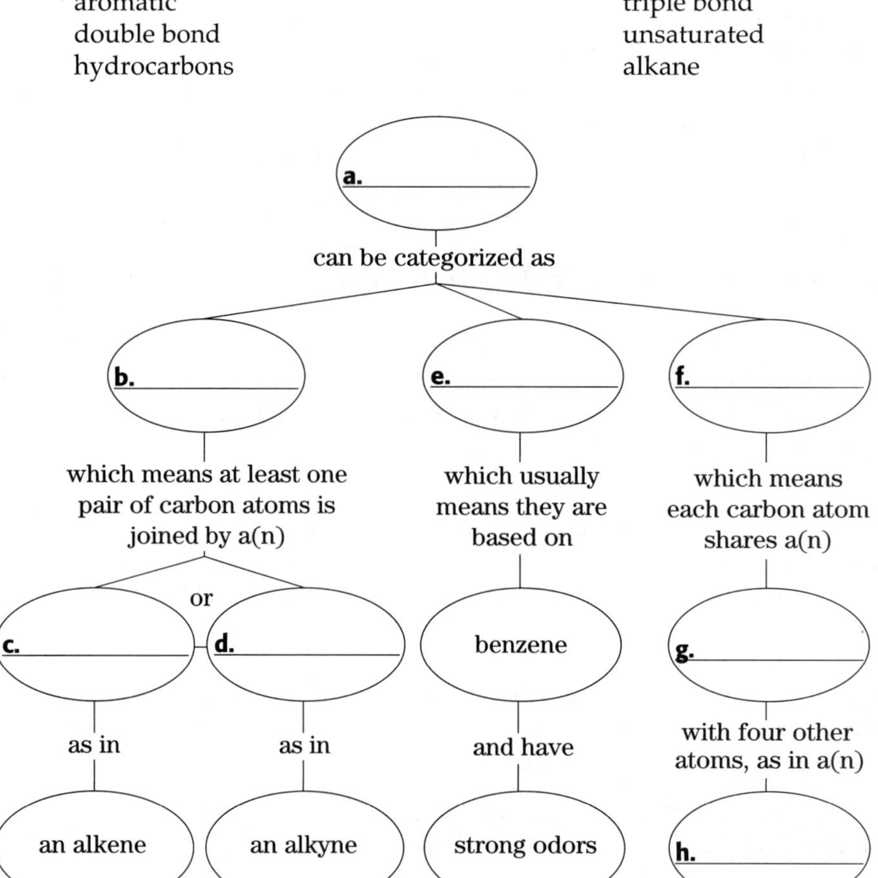

Answer:
a. hydrocarbons; b. unsaturated; c. double bond; d. triple bond; e. aromatic; f. saturated; g. single bond; h. alkane

Difficulty: 3   Section: 4   Objective: 2